WHY TO
THESE ROCKS

WHY TO THESE ROCKS

50 Years of Poems from the Community of Writers

FOREWORD BY ROBERT HASS
EDITED BY LISA ALVAREZ

Heyday, Berkeley, California

Community of Writers, Nevada City, California

Library of Congress Cataloging-in-Publication Data

Names: Alvarez, Lisa, editor. | Hass, Robert, writer of foreword. |
    Community of Writers, publisher.
Title: Why to these rocks : 50 years of poems from the Community of Writers
    / edited by Lisa Alvarez ; foreword by Robert Hass.
Description: Berkeley, California : Heyday ; Nevada City, California :
    Community of Writers, [2021]
Identifiers: LCCN 2020043307 (print) | LCCN 2020043308 (ebook) | ISBN
    9781597145299 (hardcover) | ISBN 9781597145305 (epub)
Subjects: LCSH: American poetry—21st century. | American poetry—20th
    century.
Classification: LCC PS326 .W48 2021 (print) | LCC PS326 (ebook) | DDC
    811.008/0979438—dc23
LC record available at https://lccn.loc.gov/2020043307
LC ebook record available at https://lccn.loc.gov/2020043308

Cover Art: Tom Killion, *Moonlit Sierra Pines*
Cover and Interior Design/Typesetting: Ashley Ingram

Published by Heyday
P.O. Box 9145, Berkeley, California 94709
(510) 549-3564
heydaybooks.com

Printed in Saline, Michigan, by McNaughton and Gunn

10 9 8 7 6 5 4 3 2 1

To Galway Kinnell, for his vision,
and to Lucille Clifton and C.D. Wright,
who taught and wrote poems with us for many years.

Contents

I: Over the Mountains: Poems about the Place

II: Scrupulous Mercy: Poems about Process

III: After Surfacing: Poems Produced by the Process in the Place

Foreword

Robert Hass

It's a species of bliss. Summer morning in the mountains, scintillant summer air, the vanilla and incense scent of the forest drifting through an open window or door into the living room of a ski cabin, and a group of a dozen or so poets sitting in a circle about to share drafts of poems they've written the day, or the night, before or—often enough in my case—earlier that morning.

They have been doing this, or will have been doing this, for seven mornings in a row. Reading to one another new work that they haven't really had time to have second thoughts about. Some people in the circle are quite experienced and well-published poets who have been at it a long time. Some of them are just out of college and enrolled in master's degree programs, taking a couple of years to see whether they really are writers, and learning maps of the art, and assembling first tentative manuscripts of their work. Some are middle-aged or older and just come to poetry, or are just returning to it from the busy places to which their lives have taken them. All of them are a little anxious and excited about sharing new work. Usually they begin by introducing themselves to one another. Usually the staff poet, who also has a new draft to present, welcomes them and reminds them that this is not a college creative writing class where poems are submitted to the editorial skills of the group. It's about hearing new work and spotting what's alive in it. And then they proceed. The first poet reads a poem that didn't exist the day before. The others are attentive, curious. There are usually a few minutes for the group to respond, and then a second poet reads.

If the staff poet is me, as it has often been over the years, he is feeling a small hitch at the knowledge that his own poem might seem a little dull, but the feeling is dissolved soon enough by the interest of the poems being read. The point, after all, is to see the world freshly, and being in the group allows you to be grateful that somebody got there, even if you didn't. And, of course, there is always the chance that someone will like your work better than you do, which can be helpful.

These poetry mornings at the Community of Writers have been going on in this way for more than twenty-five years. The Community itself is celebrating is fiftieth anniversary. Summer gatherings of writers have become part of the rhythm of literary life in North America, beginning, I think, with the Breadloaf Writers Conference, which was founded at Middlebury College in 1926. It was there that Robert Frost held court on summer days before the Second World War. The Community of Writers at Squaw Valley—as it was called in those early years—began in 1969. It was the first to be organized on the West Coast and was the brainchild of two novelists, Oakley Hall and Blair Fuller. The ski resort in the valley had acquired international fame by hosting the 1960 Winter Olympics. In the winter, it was one of the world's premier destinations for skiers. In summer in the 1960s and 1970s, it was a very sleepy alpine valley—a long grassy meadow with a creek running through it, horses from a riding stable grazing in the summer heat. The mass of the mountain—it was called Squaw Peak—did not match Yosemite in grandeur, but it was grand enough. The winter ski facilities and their inns were mostly empty. The hillsides and roadsides were ablaze with alpine flowers, and brown bears could be seen occasionally ambling from one forested side of the valley to the other. There was a post office. A gondola for the skiers could take hikers from the valley floor at five thousand feet to the top of the mountain at nine thousand feet, where there was a swimming pool, an ice-skating rink (left over from the Olympics), and trailheads leading into the High Sierra backcountry.

Seven miles west on the shores of Lake Tahoe, northern Californians summered, leaving the valley to itself, which made it an ideal place for writers to spend their summers. And a perfectly pleasant place, Oakley Hall and his wife, the photographer Barbara Hall, and Blair Fuller and his wife, the screenwriter Diana Fuller, thought, to gather writers for a week—novelists, essayists, playwrights, screenwriters, poets, journalists, and also editors and literary agents—to talk about their art, share work with one another, and learn something about the business side of writing novels and screenplays. Also, story had it, to party a little and play tennis. It was during this period that the town had renamed itself Olympic Valley. In summer there was a general store called Pretty Good Groceries. Over the years, the ski corporation developed the valley as a summer resort, with a faux alpine village and a mall full of shops and restaurants. It's crowded now in the summertime—jazz concerts in the evening, a kickoff event for a cycling marathon—and in the course of those years, the Community of Writers had become an institution of West Coast summers, the conferences a place for writers from all over the world, and the grocery store became Alice's Mountain Market.

The poetry program acquired its special character in the 1980s. From the outset, poets had led workshops, given lectures on craft, held manuscript conferences with beginning poets, and, if they were interested, attended the gatherings for novelists and screenwriters on how to write a sex scene or acquire an agent, skills that were arguably not so relevant to their art. So in the summer of 1985, Galway Kinnell proposed giving the poets a separate week and organizing it to emphasize making rather than critiquing or theorizing about poems or discussing the publishing business. The format was to be simple. The group assembled, wrote a draft of a poem every day, gathered every morning after the first day, and read one another their new work, say, from ten in the morning until noon. Met again at about five o'clock for a glass of wine and an informal talk about poetry and poetics by one of the poets, had dinner together, and then went off into the evening to write their next poem. On several mornings, a walk in the forest with a local naturalist, and on one afternoon, a softball game or a wildflower walk. (Midsummer is high spring in the mountains.) One night, a poetry reading by the staff poets. The participant poets would live together in the vacant ski cabins where they could talk about poetry and read each other their drafts. An administration was required, which the Hall family supplied in the person of Brett Hall Jones, the director of the Community, with the help of Lisa Alvarez, a poet and short-story writer who codirected the fiction week. Helpful young people affectionately called Elves would be hired to go from house to house mornings and pick up the poems so that they could be copied and distributed to the participants in the morning sessions by 10 a.m.

So—with occasional adjustments—this was the pattern of the Community of Writers poetry program for the last quarter of a century. In that first year, Sharon Olds joined Galway Kinnell. In the next few years, Lucille Clifton and Brenda Hillman and I joined the staff, and over the years many other poets joined the company. The central ritual—I almost wrote "its sacrament"—was the morning session, people who had fallen in love with writing poems reading one another their new poems, or the raw push toward new poems. The idea, as Galway Kinnell wrote, was that in a gathering of poets working side by side, "each poet may well break through old habits and write something stronger and truer than before." Over the years, the many poets who worked in the program had their own variations on that idea, and in the afternoon talks encouraged the group to write something stranger than before or weirder, wilder than before, or to get at their material more deeply, or to see what happens if they broke with whatever formal habits they had acquired—to take another look at the ideal of the expressive lyric, the politically engaged poem, the spiritually quiet poem, the confessional or studiously impersonal poem—in order to see what happens to their writing in an unfamiliar register. As a practical matter—seven poems in seven days—often the poets didn't so much try to make completely new kinds of poems but to make more of the kinds of poems they had been trying to write, or to make them better.

The poems in this anthology are mostly not those first raw drafts, though my guess is that quite a few of them are. One of the subjects of the afternoon talks was revision, how different poets had taught themselves to give their work a second look. My recollection is that the talks reflected a couple of ways of thinking about the process. "First take, best take," Jack Kerouac had said, or Allen Ginsberg had quoted him as saying. Some poets preferred the feel of the first flaring, and worried that you can kill the energy in a poem by trying to polish it. Other poets, reflecting a tradition extending from the Roman poet Horace to the Irish poet Yeats, would quote Yeats, who wrote, "A line will take us hours maybe / Yet if it does not seem a moment's thought / Our stitching and unstitching has been naught." And someone else would quote what Yeats wrote a few years later, "The fascination of what's difficult / has dried the sap out of my veins and rent / spontaneous joy and natural content / out of my heart." The tension between spontaneity and finish played over many of the subjects of the talks, which were the subjects on the minds of poets at the end of the twentieth century and the beginning of the twenty-first: personal experience and the subjective lyric, the confessional poem, poems of ethnic and gender identity, the impact of surrealism in American poetry, feminist poetics, social justice, privileged travel and imperialism, the postmodern critique of identity poetics, the limits of language, the relation of poetry to different spiritual traditions, the fate of the earth. After dinner, the poets returned to their work with these issues and others buzzing in their heads.

It is a pleasure to think that readers of this anthology will be replicating the experience of those summer mornings and evenings in the mountains. There are ways of reading anthologies. Some people are inclined to begin at the beginning and read straight through, absorbing the experience imagined by the editor, wanting in this case to take in the experience of this fifty years of poets trying to make fresh and spontaneous work in the art, and tracking the way that Lisa Alvarez has organized it: first work that bears on the place, then work that bears on the method, and then

work that constellates place and method—or, really, spirit—as they inter-
act with a whole set of imaginings and urgencies about what poems are
and can be. Another way, of course, is to dip in and skip around, finding a
title or a first line that arrests you, finding your way, as one does listening
to songs, into the surprising intimacy of someone else's voice speaking to
you out of their life, or a life they've imagined, or into someone else's play
with the pleasures of sound or thought, or someone else's wonder, anger,
impudence, tenderness, hurt, or joy.

Etymologically, an anthology is a collection of flowers. *Anthos* is
"flower" in Greek; it is where we get the word *anther* for the part of the
stamen of the flower that contains the pollen. Browsing an anthology, we
are pollen-gathering, as the poets were doing every day as they walked in
the high mountain air, wondering or watching where their next poem
was going to come from. From the point of view of the poet, the differ-
ence between this and the activity of bees is that the bees had not taxed
themselves with inventing the flower. And for readers the difference is—
because what we want poetry to do is to refresh our vision—not in what
happens when we read the poem but in what happens when we look up
from reading to look at the world.

Why We Return: 50 Years of the Community of Writers

Lisa Alvarez

Then why to these rocks
Do I keep coming back why,

—"The Old Moon" by Galway Kinnell

It was a Friday evening in late June. It always is. The A-frame house on Apache Court was over-full, and anyone passing by would have seen the lights and candles, and heard the laughter and music. It was one of the evenings that the poet Robert Hass captures so well in his poem "The Seventh Night." The final evening of the summer's poetry conference with some seventy or so poets gathered for one last meal together. Curry and rice, cooked in great Mexican pots on a tiny stove. Wine poured. Bread broken. Tables laid inside and out, overlooking the valley below and the patches of summer snow still scattered on the nine-thousand-foot peak of Granite Chief.

Inside, perched on the staircase that overlooked the small living room with its stone fireplace, sat Oakley Hall, novelist, master teacher, and Pulitzer Prize finalist, who helped found the Community of Writers in 1969. The A-frame was his home. He had built it himself in the late 1950s just before the 1960 Olympics came to this valley in California's Sierra Nevada. Over the many decades he, along with his wife, photographer Barbara Edinger Hall, had hosted the annual dinner, among the many gatherings the conference inspired. The poets were doing what they did every year on this evening: recitations. Not of their own work, but recitations of the poems of others, which they carried, memorized, inside them, offered as gifts, tributes on this concluding evening after a week of writing daily first drafts of poems, participants and staff alike. That night, if any faltered, losing a line or forgetting a word, other voices supplied it. Invariably the night would end with Galway Kinnell reciting Yeats's "The Lake Isle of Innisfree," but before that, the shared poems would be impossible to predict, ancient to contemporary, famous and some nearly forgotten, others unknown. For over an hour or more, the poets spoke, listened, sighed, and applauded. Oakley, on the staircase, leaned over to me and observed: "Those poets! They put such goodness into the world. It must change something."

Oakley was right.

Since its founding, the Community of Writers poetry conference has nurtured the work of generations of poets. That work has indeed changed much. Mark Strand was the first to accept Oakley's offer with a short typed response: "Sure I'll be your poet. Happily." The poets that inaugural year included Maya Angelou, Donald Justice, Galway Kinnell, Philip Levine, and Charles Wright. Kathleen Fraser, Michael McClure, and others joined the rotating staff in the decade that followed. William L. Fox became director in the late 1970s through 1983, bringing on board William Matthews, Anne Perlman, William Stafford, and many more. In those early years, poets worked alongside prose writers during the same week, but when Kinnell became director in 1985, he developed a different vision.

Poets, Kinnell believed, merited their own week, and needed to use their time in the valley to generate new work. His generative model, followed to this day, requires staff and participants to draft new poems for review in morning sessions. Kinnell persuaded Lucille Clifton, Robert Hass, Brenda Hillman, and Sharon Olds to join him, and that core staff returned year after year, strengthening the tradition and community. In those early years, Olds worked with Kinnell to shape the program. Some staff, such as Hass, who succeeded Kinnell as director, along with

Hillman, Olds, Forrest Gander, and the late C.D. Wright, spent years in the valley, developing, it turns out, a significant portion of their body of work in those early morning workshops. Some, such as Kazim Ali, Patricia Spears Jones, and Evie Shockley, arrived as participants, only to return as teaching staff. The conference has welcomed many of America's finest poets to teach, and many have contributed poems first drafted in the valley to this volume.

The participant poets who have spent a week (or two! or three! or six!) include those who have gone on to publish their work, create their own writing conferences and programs, found and edit journals, and otherwise contribute to the vibrancy of literary arts in their communities. They come from all over the country and all over the world. Not a few have become poet laureates of their cities, counties, and states. Much of the work—first forged here in a week shaped around the workshop table and around the dinner table, running the bases at the famous midweek poetry softball game or on the nature walks up Shirley Canyon, along the Truckee River and Lake Tahoe—has become published poems in journals, chapbooks, and collections, and now, some of those poems have been chosen for this anniversary anthology.

Why to These Rocks tells part of the story of the Community of Writers through work produced in the valley by both staff and participant poets, using three self-explanatory lenses: *Over the Mountains: Poems about the Place*; *Scrupulous Mercy: Poems about the Process*; and *After Surfacing: Poems Produced by the Process in the Place.* Reading them will begin to answer the question posed by Kinnell in his poem "The Old Moon" and paraphrased here: Why to these rocks do we return?

To write.

To change.

I

Over the Mountains:
Poems about the Place

LUCILLE CLIFTON

in 1844 explorers john fremont
and kit carson discovered lake tahoe

—Lodge guidebook

in 1841 Washoe children

swam like otters in the lake

their mothers rinsed red beans

in 1842 Washoe warriors began to dream

dried bones and hollow reeds

they woke clutching their shields

in 1843 Washoe elders began to speak

of grass hunched in fear and

thunder sticks over the mountain

in 1844 Fremont and Carson

highway 89 toward tahoe

a congregation

of red rocks

sits at attention

watching the water

the trees among them

rustle hosanna

hosanna

something stalls the rental car

something moves us

something moves us

something in the river

Christ

rowing for our lives

haiku

over the mountains

and under the stars   it is

one hell of a ride

SHARON OLDS

Song Before Dawn

In the dark, not the full dark,
woken by the cold, pulling the covers
up around my mouth, making a small
cavern of warmth, of living breath,
sensing the over-under of my sleep-loosened
braids—all my arms and legs
tangled around each other—I used to
lie on this mountain, and Galway and Lucille
were dreaming nearby. I used to put on
layers and layers, by touch, and despite
my fear of being outdoors in the night—
as if I were not a person but an occasion for violence—
I would go outside, the sky black,
as if, if there had been a God,
it might have petted me on the head,
like Galway in his scrupulous mercy toward me,
like my chivalry toward him,
and our confiding in each other like a child in the woods
confiding, without language, in the needles and cones.
In the dusk before first light, above
the granite domes which look from here like
peaks but are the knees and hipbone crests
and clavicles, jaws, occipital arches
under the mountains' fontanelles,

the stars are still just visible—
and in the binoculars clear and sharp—
but despite holding the heavy lenses
leaned against the stucco frame,
my tremor shows each star swiftly
whirling in a white-gold ring, like Saturn's,
in one direction, then swerving, then the other,
then an hourglass, a spiral, a bedspring—the stars
sparkler-tracing my shaking. And now,
in the quietest moment, the voice it took
the earth millions of years to speak,
the vireo before first light.
When my hands were steady, I would stand at Lucille's
shoulder at the lake, and softly pluck insects—
nine-spotted lady beetle,
giant crane fly, green darner,
black snow mosquito—off her
shoulder, nape, whitecap, and blow them
out over the glacier-blue water
toward the place where we're going, one by one,
two by two, sometimes many
at a time, someday all together, as if reunited.

ROBERT HASS

Nature Notes in the Morning

After days of wind,
No wind.
The leaves of the aspen are still.
The leaves of the alder and cottonwood,
Juddering for days and cold,
Are still.
*

East sides of the trees
Are limned with light.
Last night a stand of lodgepoles
Lit on the west side.
A kind of symmetry in days
Because they're standing still.

Just distribution theory:
Light.
*

What do I know from yesterday?
The blue bell of the gentian on the trail.
Hawk moths swarming in the scree.

Two drops of violet
In a pool of azure:
Petals of the gentian.
*

The leaves lit by light,
The rock face of the mountain gleaming.
*

And only for a second yesterday
the tanager's yellow breast.
As if the gift were excessive.

I marked the gentian's location:
At a turn in the trail, left side going up.
Right side coming down, fern shading it,
Incense cedar above it, two boulders
Of granite, mica-flecked, and I still couldn't find it
On the way back down.
*

Itō Jakuchū smeared a paste of egg yolk
And white paint on the back of his scrolls
And then crushed oyster shell to another paste
And added carmine for the rooster's crest
He painted into the soft silk.

Smuggled Prussian blues from Europe
For the way light looked on plums.
*

Values in the right place: a country
That outlaws the use of Prussia blue.
*

Lists of colors to ban from future kingdoms:
(Make list here).
(Terre verte, alizarin).

*

Lips: carmine.
Last streaks of sunset: alizarin.

*

The old art historian. I was going on
About Cezanne and he took me into the studio
And took down four tubes of shades of green
And stood me in front of an easel with a brush
And said, "Now, put these on paper
In small rectangular daubs so that they shimmer,
And until you can do that, I say this
In all friendship, shut up about Cezanne."

*

That was—what?—thirty years ago.
Professor Henry Shaeffer-Simmern.
Trained at Bauhaus. Escaped the Nazis in 1939.
He wore bow ties and plaid shirts, wrote about perception.
Big man, full of vitality.
He must be long dead.

*

Sierra morning.
Bright sun. No wind,
So that stirring in the cottonwood
Must be a warbler.

AL YOUNG

In the Sierras

for Oakley and Barbara Hall

Way up here, where sky comes close
to calling all the shots, where
photographers, geographers and gopher-
loathing golfers and creature-comfort joggers,
where bikers, hikers, wrecking crews and
hoarse writers alike mount slow invasions;
here, where whole fields, whole hills heal
and mountains make big money mean,
peace speaks its native tongue.

Way up here, where sky comes close,
where stakes grow vast, where the last
and first run neck and neck, where loveliness
lays herself on every line at once;
up here, where far and close dissolve,
where the Sierras do not err and terror
cheapens. Sleeplessness like formlessness
must nest at midnight-lighted height.
Peace gets and takes its chances.

DEAN YOUNG

Dear Bob,

The mountain thinks it's the same
without you but it's wrong. Maybe
the same stars whisking themselves
further off, the darker the brighter,
same chamomile crushed underfoot
but the little, wiry dog we loved
has preceded us into paradise, not
that I expect to join her even though
my own crappy heart's worse, running's
out but I may be finally learning how
to sit in a chair. I still don't know
what to call the good morning bird
although whatever word'd be no truer
than manzanita. I think namelessness
has a crush on me, on how clean
I keep my room, the usual stunned
ruckus of wake up. But it's a different
moon, different woman on the hotel balcony
yet the same kinda scary, vacant stare,
caryatid foreseeing what? Before
turning back to the customary, immaculate
vacation squalor inside. The cash machine
still says "enter to exit" but there's
more water in the creek than I've ever seen,
the brighter the darker, in that first dream
there was none.

CORNELIUS EADY

Time Out

We didn't grow up to be team players:
The wordy ones, the shy ones, the smart-ass ones,
The ones who burned alone, or in small groups,
Who had this tic, or far-away look, or dreamed
While wide-awake, too fat, too thin; too dark
Or poor, or aware of our
bodies; too restless
Or lazy or uncoordinated; in a word, doomed.

So here we are on a baseball field, in sunny July,
In Tahoe City, CA, in middle of a week of writing,
Back at Squaw Valley, our poems sleep,
For a day; our memories, and longings and angers,
Our struggle with how to put it down, get it right,
Our nagging with the truth set gently aside.

Tell me a grander beauty than a game; the heat,
The dust, the slow rolling of hours, our bodies
Learning the swing, or remembering the last time
Our muscles spoke in that combination. Teamed up,
Anxious as raw recruits,

Who counts the swings? How many outs?
Who knows the score? Who tracks the innings?
And we swing, we poets, and we miss, and we drop.
O perfect summer day, when no one loses.

Harryette Mullen

from *Tanka Diary*

The botanical garden is just as I remember,
although it is certain that everything
has changed since my last visit.

How many hilarious questions these fuzzy
fiddleheads are inquiring of spring
will be answered as green ferns unfurl?

Walking the path, I stop to pick up
bleached bark from a tree, curled into
a scroll of ancient wisdom I am unable to read.

Even in my dreams I'm hiking
these mountain trails expecting to find a rock
that nature has shaped to remind me of a heart.

KATIE FORD

Still Life

Down by the pond, addicts sleep
on rocky grass half in water, half out,
and there the moon lights them
out of tawny silhouettes into the rarest
of amphibious flowers I once heard called *striders*,
between, but needing, two worlds.
Of what can you accuse them now,
                    beauty?

KEVIN YOUNG

The light here leaves you

The light here leaves you
lonely, fading

as does the dusk
that takes too long

to arrive. By morning
the mountain moving

a bit closer to the sun.

This valley belongs
to no one—

except birds who name
themselves by their songs

in the dawn.
What good

are wishes, if they aren't
used up

The lamp of your arms.
The brightest

blue beneath the clouds—

We guess
at what's next

unlike the mountain

who knows it
in the bones, a music

too high
to scale.

The burnt, blurred world

The burnt,
blurred world

where does it end—

The wind
kicks up the scent

from the stables
where horseshoes hold

not just luck, but
beyond. But

weight. But a body

that itself burns,
begs to run.

The gondola quits just
past the clouds.

The telephone poles
tall crosses in the road.

Let us go
each, into the valley—

turn ourselves
& our hairshirts

inside out, let the world
itch—for once—

Black like an eye

Black like an eye

bruised night brightens
by morning, yellow

then grey—
a memory.

What the light was like.

All day the heat a heavy,
colored coat.

I want to lie
down like the lamb—

down & down
till gone—

shorn of its wool.
The cool

of setting & rising
in this valley,

the canyon between us
shoulders our echoes.

Moan, & make way.

The sun's small fury

The sun's small fury
feeds me.

Wind dying down.

We delay, & dither
then are lifted

into it, brightness
all about—

O setting.
O the music

as we soar
is small, yet sating.

What you want—

Nobody, or nothing
fills our short journeying.

Above even the birds,
winging heavenward,

the world is hard
to leave behind

or land against—
must end.

I mean to make it.

Turning slow beneath
our feet,

finding sun, seen
from above,

this world looks
like us—mostly

salt, dark water.

It's death there

It's death there
is no cure for

life the long
disease.

If we're lucky.

Otherwise, short
trip beyond.

And below.

Noon,
growing shadow.

I chase the quiet
round the house.

Soon the sound—

wind wills
its way against

the panes. Welcome
the rain.

Welcome
the moon's squinting

into space.
The trees

bow like priests.

The storm lifts
up the leaves.

Why not sing.

CATHY PARK HONG

Loupe

using jeweler's magnifying glass, like a monocle
we look at a common weed flower—tattered
      to lace by aphids,
distracted, the blue blazing down, towering spruce—
recalling the museum
& looking through the microscope
to see a micromosaic of birds made of butterfly
scales, silvery
      like your aunt's enameled chest
the mosaic of abalone
      a tough white meat,
old women in a small island made a livelihood
diving for abalone
      gearless, in black rubber
stalwart mermaids.
Visiting this island, your family feasted on this
bland tough
      delicacy butterflied on a platter
afterwards, outside
look up at the windows of the restaurant
      wait staff settling
down feasting on your family's leftovers

MATTHEW ZAPRUDER

Poem for Coleridge

The lake was super fucking cold,
and with every smallest
increment got colder. I plunged
my head. Under no sound.
Not even extreme silentness.
No stupid ideas, no words
of comfort I should not
or not have not said, not my
constant horrible ungrateful
desire to have different form
or be done. All this talking.
Not even breath. Everyone
was really gone. There is no
word for that x. Under
it outwaits time. Later on shore
wrapped in a white towel and still
feeling ridiculous and also
a little secretly proud for having
so mortally scared myself
I would say some mystical
inexorable communion feeling
toward those ancient blue

waters pulled me, meaning
I had already forgotten, I was
as always already talking too much
to keep away something numberless.

FORREST GANDER

Madonna del Parto

And then smelling it,
feeling it before
the sound even reaches
him, he kneels at
cliff's edge and for the
first time, turns his
head toward the now
visible falls that
gush over a quarter
mile of uplifted sheet–
granite across the valley
and he pauses,
lowering his eyes
for a moment, unable
to withstand the
tranquility—vast, unencumbered,
terrifying, and primal. That
naked river
enthroned upon
the massif altar,
bowed cypresses
congregating on both
sides of sun-gleaming rock, a rip
in the fabric of the ongoing

forest from which rises—
as he tries to stand, tottering, half–
paralyzed—a shifting
rainbow volatilized by
ceaseless explosion.

KAZIM ALI

The Failure of Navigation in the Valley

to C.D. Wright

No body is fixed in position no one can be known

Still I am read by satellites my tendency extrapolate

In the mountains I have no GPS I don't know where to go

There are those trees their leaves flicker like little jewels a whole bucketful

Darkness stares back are you even human anymore

I close the curtains at night not because I think others will see in

Turn left there but so I do not see the reflection that is pure dark

I am not afraid of anything oh is that so

Citizen bear do this place not belong to you

Unseen I wander through the thorny place of what I no that ain't it

No fear can be knew can be none fuck how do you spell it

I held a heavy jade pendant in my hand once not in this valley in another

In the range of limited human experience how many places are there really

I don't even have to look at the earth anymore I just have to listen

Now that hillbilly whisper guides me which way to turn how far up the
      turn is

Drawling like moonshine we're really off the grid now

Making wild prayers to the green dark which kind do you mean

Thank god we thought of her recording this voice both kinds

Victoria Dalkey

In Fear of Mountains

Resinous as wine
the pine's scent steals
through the window. Outside

mountains recall the musculature
of male anatomy—abdominals braided like baskets,
deltoids of polished graphite.

Honestly
I hate mountains, fear them as flatlanders did,
panicking at the dark recesses,

ridiculous strength.
They give nothing, hold themselves
in, scarifying

as the trip with father high
into the darkest pines, past train sheds
at Norden, then the plunge

to the highway pawnshop to redeem
his gold watch, cufflinks,
tie tack and ring, the whole time

my fingers gripping a pencil—
drawing a house with many windows
each one hung
with lace curtains.

Dan Bellm

Aspens

The individual life is not the point—*admire me*
I am a violet, and so on, as John Keats mocked,
in the voice of the self who wants to be more precious
than existence—long parentless by then,
nursing his brother Tom through the long bloodcoughing
months of death and knowing his own could come soon,
perhaps before love, or another visitation of poetry,
though he had only reached the Chamber of Maiden-thought
in the house of many rooms he was sketching out
in his own faint light—*on all sides many doors set open but all*
dark all leading to dark passages—maybe few to be revealed
in an individual life. So the naturalist led us poets
up a creekbed to show us a tiny portion of our own world:
a fragile meetingpoint of volcanic rock & granite
that over a hundred thousand years urged forth a way
for water to wash down and make this canyon to the valley:
told us that the grove of quaking aspens we stopped beside
ought to call into question our definition of a tree:
not separate trees but clones sprung from an underground
rhizomal oh I don't know what the word was,
which makes me ashamed—I didn't write it down—as if
knowledge of the names of things means understanding anything
of what they are—the other poets, I figured, were writing down
notes for me—wanting really to have the labeled placards
in an arboretum (*dote upon me I am a primrose*) so I could

walk away satisfied knowing more than enough but actually
nothing much. The point was that the system of roots beneath us
was vaster than we could think, a million years old or so,
and apparently so capable of continuing sending up clones each season
that it can wait for the arrival of the next ice age to this valley
if it takes another million years, and the theorizers who know
that our minds and words stop short of what this might mean
have posited what they can only call "theoretical immortality."
(All of the poets wrote *that* one down.) All right, so I returned
to poetry so late, guilty, ashamed, regretful, sad, all right.
My teacher beside me—disoriented by all these
lateblooming Sierra wildflowers unknown in northern New Hampshire—
another system but not another earth—connected underneath—
(same late-July mosquitoes here as there biting me though,
taking me back to my summers by Mt. Chocorua at the commie camp,
swimming in the deep pond there, deciding to be a writer and so
to change the world, *rich in the simple worship of a day*)—she said
she was grateful there was such a community of writers as this one
and she had found it—so little of the usual mutual hatred
and self-mistrust because we're working every day and facing
the blankness of paper, urging each other on, not showing off our
bundles of poems from home to be doted upon or angling
for career moves, though I do want my fucking book to get out
of my house. She agreed with me, no, you are not, at the age
of 45, the next young thing the poetry biz is waiting
to discover, and you can thank God herself for it, having had
students at the age of 23 all but drown in acclaim and felt
afraid for them as in, O honey—just wait until you're in
a small town somewhere with an underpaying job and a couple of
babies, not enough time, a husband who helps out, or not,
and one book on the shelf while the world has moved on

to the next bright morning star—that's when, if you're lucky,
you'll be a writer. Send down your taproot then, into the
many-chambered whatever it is, the comfort and fright of it,
that we're all connected. *And thus by every germ of Spirit*
sucking the Sap from mould ethereal every human might become great,
and Humanity instead of being a wide heath of Furse and Briars
with here and there a remote Oak or Pine, would become
a grand democracy of Forest Trees. These plant "communities"—
manzanita, huckleberry, snow-something, oh I didn't write those down
either I was so tired, the words are not the point—they're migrating
over geological time—they send messages to each other
across the great spongeous rootmass about changes in temp. and
rainfall, outbreaks of blight, accumulated experience we'd call
gossip or history, the sports and weather, film at 11—they slowly
move, and so others move with them, what's the choice—the point
is the interwoven indistinguishableness that all life feeds
and is fed by, not the individual life. And the hope
that I will be communicated with among the forms of life
must be what is meant by a blessing—say, the man I saw
laying his hands on another man's head, in the rain, to bless him,
in a crowd at the corner of Post & Stockton in the middle of the day—
it must be only our bodies, our skin, that makes us think
we're contained in one place in one self, as a tree appears to end
at the root, the rock, the leaf-edge, the air, as a mountain appears
to end at the level ground, so we need the laying on
of hands to make an entryway into the one
oh what will I call it? We don't even have the same desires
as ourselves, as when the ex-President said, "I have opinions
of my own. Strong opinions. But I don't always agree with them."
We are temporary shadows constantly turning around
to misremember, elaborate constructions

unrecoverable a moment later, contradictory lifelines
in the palms of our hands. So even a sad song causes happiness
when it comes from the heart. So Jacob asked a blessing of his father
as I did, though I too had to steal it, holding his hand as he died
in a coma in a narrow bed: still, I think he was waiting for me.
And afterwards we go on living, at our own mercy,
which can be short at hand. Am I too old?
I am not the next young thing but that has never stopped
the subterranean-stream-continuation of all the desires.
Band of rose gold on my finger, and 16 years of marriage
to the man I love, faithful in our quotes open relationship
well are we? though openness can be an aperture or chasm. The man
handing me change in the hardware store with my wall-grabbers
and wingnuts had two nipple rings, which I thought was one
too many, and was young enough to be my child; he made me hot
as our hands met though it meant nothing much, and am I too old
to get a nipple ring? I want to ask him if I did that would it
hurt, but a part of me I love is afraid it might not hurt enough:
more unfulfillment in desire, even the desire for pain, which runs on
in the underground stream and resurfaces each season
in its fashion, as here in a brightly-lit store midday
on Castro St.: I wanted to lick the salt from his skin.
Oh what would I turn into if I were single again? The devious
frightened loner I was before. Undiscovered by poetry.
Now we look upward on the trail because the life of birds,
living or ornamental, this one or the birds of tapestry in the decor
of our minds, the nothing that is not there, and the nothing
that is—their life is song. A junco but I didn't see it,
the guide helped us notice and then I heard it, a scold, a
trailing-off *compleynt*, as Bela Bartók must have heard
the actual Hungarian birds of his youth that he lived among

before the disaster of our midcentury dispersed the forms of life
but how did he still hear them and place them
directly by their song and without names into that never-quite-
finished Piano Concerto No. 3, his cry of anguished love
and a capitulation before some wellspring he knew would continue
after him, or at any rate that's what I heard when I first
heard it in Ann Arbor some twenty years ago, the days when I
was almost giving up on my own soul and living in that piss
smelling boarding house on Miller Avenue, mourning my first lover,
smoking so much dope, back in the closet again,
romanticizing Larry and Sadie the drunks from the U.P. next door
because they were Indians and had done so much Real Time
in the Washtenaw County Jail right across the street—
we heard the screams and fighting of the prisoners at night—
and who therefore seemed to live more intensely, have *more* life,
than one such as me writing termpapers on *Middlemarch*,
when what I wanted from them really was another sedative drug—
what a sorrowful young youth I was, pitiful jade plant in my window
likewise half in love with death, but I had a rainsoaked *Book of
Nightmares* and *A Love Supreme* and the birds that Bela Bartók conjured up
for me, one mortal body passing the song on to another
across indefinite time, his final music, so full of legend and glory,
sitting on a cot an almost penniless refugee in 1945 on W. 57th St.
in New York knowing he was dying, racing to leave it
as a birthday present for his wife and even more, a useful
concert-piece that she could go on playing and earn a little
money from to make her way, the sheet music found only later
lying out of order on every available surface of bed and desk
and floor, a windowless room in which he caused
the birds of gone-forever Hungary to go on singing.

JOHN HARVEY

Out of Silence

How the light diffuses round house corners;
redwood walls, the breaking colour of packed earth,
ochre in the mouth.

The red woodpecker testily chiselling sap from a small ash
the only sound in the valley.

SHARON OLSON

Running the Bases

The first-base coach tells her to run on anything.
The third-base coach smiles, says, *how did you get here?*

The journey had been effortless
because she really did not remember running,
as if she had not paid attention to detail, again.

She dared not look back,
the runners were piling up behind her, one by one.
The opposing team members were eager to embrace her,
and she could feel herself tempted by comfort, and betrayal.

But her father, and brother, standing outside the bases,
had guided her this far, and she felt nothing
like debt, or honor, only warmth, as if
the words, and the smile were more than a gesture:
Listen to us, they said, *and you will be safe
no matter what happens, for you have learned
about the journey you will make to the riverside
where the boat is waiting, the arms around you,
the final letting go.*

*In this moment look around you at this outfield,
this infield, write down what you remember
before you leave to come home.*

MOLLY FISK

Kindness

for Tad

Half-way through our nap the rain begins, hits the window,
plashes through the double-needled pines, and splurts down

onto the mule's ears and rein orchids, the clustered blue-faced
penstemons, sinking without a trace into the granite soil.

I roll gently out from under his arm and watch him sleeping the sleep
of the sunburned, of the good son, the wall-primer and painter,

the sleep of a man who is truly tired and knows someone
loves him, since I unaccountably began to cry about it over lunch

and couldn't stop, watching him eat was suddenly
too much for me, thinking how easily he could have died

in that fall, how he wandered lonely in the wilderness of his own mind,
never mind that people cared for him, for so long, twenty years,

long enough for me to get my second wind, to begin again
to grow up, so that I recognized true love when I saw it, looked

beyond the gnarled teeth and broken nose, the central, longitudinal scar
that runs his length from trachea to pubis, beyond the lost names

and repeated stories into kindness, so that when he began the steep
climb out of his brainpan's maze into stronger light, how lucky

I was there at the top of the stairs, passing by.

CHRIS DAVIDSON

Leaving the Poets

When we part, we reel in our blazing tongues
to say our *so longs* in the plain speech.
Some will board jets and be lifted, as joy,
always darting out of view, briefly lifts the heart.
Others will drive, fanning across the geography.
I will arrive south, out of the mountains and cross
irrigated plains, descending into a landscape
of light and sprawl, hemmed in by the Pacific,
beneath an overwhelming humidity of smog
and song. In that place where I was raised
to see in the future money, how to drive in lanes,
to dive beneath waves holding my breath,
to sing without being heard but seen,
how to pray, I'll remember, I hope,
that for a while I was mainly a pedestrian.
I slept among conifers and above a torrent.
An animal each morning woke me
with a sound like a submerged train.
I drank till late with makers of wine,
houses, pavilions, battles. No one need know this
to say goodbye. As in the story of Jacob
in the desert wrestling through the whole night,
this parting is not about knowledge:
we grapple with true love, then we limp away.

When we kiss, our mouths fall one to another
like the burning coal the angel touched
to the prophet's lips, who then had new news
and a voice altered for its articulation.
When we kiss, with imperfect organs
of disclosure, we touch histories. So.
So long.

NANCY CHERRY

A Poet's Errand

The trouble with poetry is
it's either subjective or objective.

—Basho

At the junction of Highway 89 and the road
back, I pull over, get out of the borrowed car
and sit at the foot of a high-wire tower,
its white foot bolted to the earth.
It is hot in the parking lot where
folks pull in for 7-Eleven or
the bicycle shop—its tangle of spokes
and tires—before turning to the mountain where
cumulus-nimbus canter to the gate. Drivers,
blind with the afternoon glare
and parking-lot dust, press in for a space.
They need directions and something
cold to drink. I hum with the electric tension
of PG&E's galvanized substation—
the conductors, transformers and end-of-July heat.
Tonight no one gets to sleep.

CHARLES DOUTHAT

More Than Mountains

Wasn't our first question whether the map
could be trusted? And didn't we set out to test it
by following to the source one of those silver

snow-melt streams that wrinkled down a side canyon,
feeding the green river in the long canyon below?
And isn't that why we forded it that morning,

barefoot with our boots tied around our necks,
and climbed the dusty switchbacks
until our knees ached and our heels blistered

and our t-shirts stuck to the smalls of our backs?
And didn't we keep climbing when the trail left off—
losing sight of the stream often—by following

the downhill, trickling, water-sound that finally
led us up to a field of bear grass and an alpine lake
walled in by rockslides loosed from the peaks above?

And why weren't we satisfied to rest there and swim
instead of filling our canteens, circling the lake
and plotting the next leg of our climb?

Did we both have the same idea—being young enough
and well-equipped—of reaching a peak that day?
Or did one persuade the other that the last leg

would be an easy scramble over raw boulders
once we left the hampering brush behind?
It wasn't, but when we got to the first high ridge—

both of us gasping, hearts pumping, half dizzy
under the breathless, western sky—
didn't you want to go on as I did?

And wasn't a higher one waiting for us
and then a third further on where we finally stopped,
realizing the ridges might go on and on

without certainty of height ever being established
by us at least, our judgments already distorted
by thin air, by the metallic, high-altitude light?

Yet wasn't this summit what we'd aimed for,
this being above and yet surrounded
by mountains going off into mountains,

folding over and down into a distance dappled
by more and everlasting mountains?
What was the restlessness then, the necessity
that stood us up against our exhaustion,
that set us casting about, kicking and knocking loose
random stones on the flat of our ridge?
What were we dreaming of more than mountains?

What in the stones made us gather them
first into a ring, then a cairn, then an upright shape

that gradually took on the appearance of a man?
Remember the horizontal slab I found for shoulders
and the squared-off block you placed for the head?

Didn't we try our best to make a standing man
and to face him west, returning the sun's late gaze?
And in raising him up didn't you find yourself

naming this figure in your mind, as I did?
And later, burnt-out, sweat-chilled, half-staggering
down hard ridges into valley twilight,

didn't other names occur to you as well,
word-forms that tumbled out of the mountains
as things do at dusk, taking shape suddenly

from nothing, then falling back, reabsorbed?
Did you think the names would never be forgotten?
Yet do you remember even half of them now

half as well as you do our cold camp that night,
or the next-day muscle ache, or the morning forest light
you called breakfast light, as pale

and washed out as the green half-tones of the map
we carried all that summer, unfolding it
and refolding it until the creases finally tore?

NOAH BLAUSTEIN

American Thrush: Search and Rescue

I've been thinking about theories
of collective unconsciousness, trying
to will the 11,832 foot peak that
dead ends this valley to move a little
so I can see the meadow behind—mule's ear,
dusky horquilla, drought spring—
and the base camp of my late teens. The man-boy
there, above tree line, lightness
of thin air, so thin Carlos, furloughed
from juvie to learn alpine rescue,
rolls into me in his mummy bag, "I haven't
told anyone this yet." "What?" "I stabbed
someone the night before we came out here,
I stabbed them real bad." "Is there
any other way," I asked, "to stab
someone?" and he didn't laugh and I watched
him sleep all starlight and in the morning
we rope-coursed a cliff face to pull a woman
with broken coccyx out of an ice pick shoot,
to replace the adrenaline of guilt
with the adrenaline of risk. Tonight
I want the mountain to shift a little
to the left so I can watch John Muir
walk away from his rigid Protestant
Scot father, so I can watch him

pioneer woods and cliffs, unknown
flora, unknown fauna, at night,
moon, no moon, water oozle, no oozle,
with his dog Stickeen and remember
what it was like not to back down
to fear, to the things that might happen
and the things one "should" do. But
in these ski slope condos without snow,
in the minds of the chickadees, the collective
unconscious is elsewhere tonight. My friend
puts his daughter to bed with a bottle
of milk. Her second word after Cooper, the dog,
was "terrorist," and I can hear someone watching
a documentary on the Ambush at the River of Secrets,
another battle in another War of Secrets. At any moment,
one out of every four people in this country
is concentrating on Jesus showing up
within the year, and I'm giving up
on the mountain to call a friend
who won't get the mail because it could
contain a new flu and then I will
join 5.6 million other Americans watching
their favorite ex-model host a cooking show,
make ceviche and marvel how an old,
overweight fiction writer, 87
million Muslims once wanted to kill
got to bed her, bravely, every night.

Farnaz Fatemi

Playing Softball after 21 Years

My bones shake themselves out
as I take first steps onto the borrowed mountain field

two decades after you dragged me to my first game. Linked-arm lover
under redwood grove. Your gaze clay.

I stand at the outfield grass and look at the pines past the line of the
        fence. I feel
tall and steely, closer to twenty than sixty. My limbs hold me in place.

So young still. My knees aren't creaky. I chase fly balls. I know this
        feeling
won't last. I punch the leather of my glove. I wish you'd made 40.

Two other poets in right field—we're stretching the rules—are talking
about a form one is experimenting with. I have that prayerful longing

to never forget this moment. They're almost as young as we were.
Can you come play here, she says, pointing to 2nd. *I have no idea what to do.*

I jog over. You would have been proud, too. I am playing softball with
        poets.
How are you not hanging at this fence, laughing when I tap the ball
        towards 3rd

and arc my way to 1st? I am all grins when my heel hits the rubber. Safe.
Your teeth were so big and it's easy to remember.

Look at the treetops and see how thin the air is. Watch a hawk on a high
    current.
I was so lucky you loved me. I make it to third, my legs humming

your name and I think it doesn't matter how this game ends. The runner
    at first is
doubled off because she runs on a fly ball. I am disappointed.

But today I see what you saw when you coaxed me to play. I was 24 and
    my flesh
hugged my tendons and my bones and was soaked in what had been
    coming

for what seemed like forever and my legs held strong and my body
    unfurled
and the promise you made was that all of it was already in me. You were
    right.

My body is still mine, at least a little longer. And it is back with you
under the evening lights of that city park in late spring, damp air on our
    necks

and redwood trees in our noses on the drifting breeze.

Karen Terrey

Why Does Godzilla Have to Die?

My nephew's head is monstrous he says
so we practice nodding my freakishly small head
forward and his back in the frame for our selfies.
He says you can never have enough selfies
and I don't know what he means.
He's an expert on Godzilla,
glad they reinstated the fire breathing
from the original. In the movie, Godzilla grabs
the monster's insect-beak mouth and
pries it open, forces a beam of flame down its throat
until it collapses into a blackened corpse
at Godzilla's prehistoric stumpfeet.
With my nephew, everything is young.
We discover the beaten-down track
high in Donner Canyon where the Stevens Trail
climbed in 1844. Here's our selfie
at the secret plaque. We look for wagon wheel ruts
in the stone. When did the pioneers know
they couldn't turn back?
Everything is living only once
and yet here a seeping spring
has raised horsetail fronds
the last pioneer walking behind the last wagon
paused to run his hand across.

How could they not keep going?
Everyone arrives at a foreign country,
even Godzilla. How he killed the monster
was strangely intimate. When Joe was a toddler
and Godzilla died he screamed NO!
and threw his toy Godzilla across the room
where it hit my father's new wife.
Compassion is a slippery thing
always breaking like a yolk
without a shell. Someone hung metal wind chimes
to the roof of the snow sheds
protecting the train tracks
and Joe fears the mournful ringing
through the shadowed tunnels.
We run as far as we can
in the bars of sound to the edge
of an old darkness. It is very windy.

JENNIFER GIVHAN

The Cheerleaders

If you have not written your cheerleader poem,
they're good for many things.

—The Writers' Conference

I want to defend the cheerleaders
to those who've said it was anti-feminist
here at the mountain camp

in the Sierra Nevadas among the Jeffrey pine
with its bark that smells of vanilla and
the same Bailey's Irish Cream I first tasted

in high school, at a party—
these girls are rural and white, too young
for sex to be sexualized, bright pink

blooming bows in their hair, tightly coiled
with immaculate white woven through
their chanting as if in ecstasy

everything, here among the white-
flowered cat paws that lay close to the ground
each cold summer night then rise

toward the sun come noon, the cheerleaders
shout for themselves, but at home,
for the team, for the boys, toward

the moon—the way I was a cheerleader
in the Southwestern desert twenty minutes
from the Mexicali border in the egg

frying summer heat, and my boyfriend
after spooning me all day in the guest bed
at his nana's would drive me to practice—

I'd fit my thick thighs into lycra-tight shorts,
pull taut my dark hair and bother anyway with bronze
Covergirl foundation and glittered purple eyeliner

though I'd sweat it all off in an hour
of basing basket tosses, of being the one to lift
another girl freer than me, the one who kept

flying girls from falling to packed-earth, scorched
dirt below our white and silver gel-inspired
ASICS training shoes with flexible soles for dancing—

but one girl flew to the left of our interlocked
crisscrossed arm basket and we couldn't catch her
before she landed on her side, on her chest, palms

down but she didn't break any bone
or the baby we found three weeks later
sprouting like a flower beneath her bruised ribcage.

I want to defend these girls in the tall grass
with their backs to the lake with their black
and red skirts like fringed ballet tutus

or costume burlesque, their cheer faces
like masks I'd put on and practice
when my mother asked why I was moody

and what were the bruises purpling my arms
my hips my thighs. What's not feminist
about this, how the sport could send us—

most of whom had never been on a plane
since there was no airport in our town
besides barns for crop dusters—

to New York City. It's not recklessness or
drunkenness but the culture, its lack
of options, how I wanted to dance

where there were no dance schools
where the only art was sprayed on the bellies
of walls where resistance meant

disobeying our parents meant breaking
curfew meant bonfires in barrels
meant sex between sweet-smelling stacks

of alfalfa beside hay bales beside ditchwater.
I want to defend these cheerleaders
in their sassy and hopeful irreverent poses

how Nietzsche says metaphor is desire
to be somewhere else, how the cheerleaders
are likewise, the pouty lips they taught us

openly mocked, the meanest of us
the toughest the loudest to cheer
remind me still of the pinecones that'll stay

closed with pitch until hit with fire
then open, that need damage, some seeds
need a bit of abuse before they can germinate

like forest freeze, like fire, an animal's gut,
these serotinous cones that the lodgepole pine
give of themselves to be hurt—like the cheerleaders

of my girlhood, of the *go!* of the *big blue!*—
they aren't thinking of this or of anything
as they lift toward the sky and take root.

ANDREW ALLPORT

All Nature Will Fable,

Wrote Thoreau, if you lack ability
to express it in language, every rock's shine

shimmers into myth. Thus armed, our father
& son go fishing a pond below the railroad cut,
bright bobbers lacquered in a green slime.

An osprey folds its wings and bombs
into the water, rising with a tremble

as a Reno-bound freight train thunders by
above, machine in the garden.

Which machine? Which Garden?
When there was no more beauty, we decided
we could worship the loss of beauty, & so
nothing was lost. Lo, how the water sparkled

under the uranium mine, clear as lucite,
the sky a monument to ignorance.

Monofilament in the bushes along the shore,
seabirds dying of thirst. Mommy and me
saw it once. Did you see sharks? Yes, some,

I lie. And where was me? You? An egg
we carried in our pale adaptation
of a mystery. You were one

conclusion in the middle of a line,
mine story, the end of life as we knew.

CHRISTINA HUTCHINS

Coming Down the Mountain

Last night the Milky Way draped its plush
ribbon, random light, as ever it does.
So often the radiance masked,
in this high valley we are discovered
by light come as if to seek us.

What is between you and me? Is it light, too?
Warmth. Voices. Legacies of violence. Our seeking
and being sought for, and the want of that. Sometimes
poets reading each other's poems pretend
the thing between them is only a poem.

I had felt the turn into a one o'clock wind on the longest
day of the year, frothing of Aspen boughs in sun,
the seeking wheels of a bicycle under a girl
who stood to press harder up the hill,
spokes of galaxies glittering.

I had wanted to ride the gondola, to hike
up for the dip down and sway, cliffs and crevices,
a granite face, and the shadow of a hand on a page.
Maybe I wanted to let the mountain long for me a little.
To know brute beauty reaching for me.

But I grew lost. I climbed and climbed,
up without a trail, feet and hands and bad decisions,
arrived on Broken Arrow, the wrong summit,
and trying to descend, there came a cliff. My body
bore itself back to the top, and my whole life was alone.

Crossing a scree patch, I had set my foot
against a weathered log, a stout sea-lion,
my arms could not have grappled it. A soft kick,
tap of the toe, a little human weight,
and down it rolled, not stopping.

I was clinging to Manzanita,
and the big, twice-dead thing, accelerating down,
down the face of the mountain, bounced and sprung
against rock outcroppings, and tumbled out of sight.
That could have been me.

We spin the edge of a galaxy, alive
by a necessary search between us, mattering
each other forth. But that spinning log—
the mountain, impersonal as sea in storm, cared nothing.
I ate snow, packed my water bottles with snow.

Then there was nowhere else to go,
and when I had to put my foot to a bit of unmoored
granite and the gruss gave way, our steady world
could not hold. It was I, the silver log, accelerating,
tumbling. Loose matter.

Don't steal my bones.
They are worth nothing to you.

A tiny old pine. I rolled into it, and I clung.
Hours later, descended, I found the trail,
and darkness came complete, and cold.
I sat down on the path and waited. The Milky Way
could not find ground amid the pines.

But our lamps are stars. How glad: three
lights, jagging among boulders, bobbing through
trunks and branches, herald three voices
shouting my name. How glad I was to see, be sought,
to be found, to close my eyes and be embraced.

JENNIFER SWANTON BROWN

A Difficult Subject

Mountains scare me.
I've told you before, but you
don't believe me.

There is no place to lie down.
Even with a yellow door.

The ants are very big,
dogs run off leash, barking,
big dogs.

The stairs are uneven,
Some wobble.
The piano is missing.

I can't breathe when I swim.
The horizon is over my head.
Even when I'm alone, you are
always here.

If I want a bear, it is a spider.
Picture frames and light switches
hang crooked and resist.

A dog sleeps in my bed,

my throat opens and closes.

I found an entire six pack of Bud Light.

I had to drink.

I have too many keys.

I found someone else's birth control pills.

Flies fly in the shower,

(which could happen anywhere.

Here it is your fault.)

Did you know there are golf balls?

Your name starts with a Z.

I followed the rules and still hate.

I am almost over it.

Mountains scare me.

The water is you calling.

SUSAN COHEN

Natural History

It seemed natural to be alive back then.

—Jack Gilbert

If there is a place where being alive
seems natural, it should be here
in the bright gravity of a mountain,
its hollows still wet with snow in June.
Sunset rouges the clouds.
Somewhere near, a stream
goes about its enterprise.
Wind sizes up some sugar pines
while a bug takes me for natural,
landing to nurse on my salt.
Once, I sat on a ledge above a valley,
faced by an immensity of peaks.
I was alive but momentary,
relieved at the size of my unimportance.
Back then, I mostly sat in cafes
complaining life was hard
when life was hardly anything.
Those friends are gone.
To be somewhere between sky
and dirt seems enough now that death
feels more and more natural.

The mountain is alive tonight, full
of stream sounds and bats. A dog barks.
The spring snow that dazzled me
melts into the dark.

Marci Vogel

In the Olympic village   tiny constellations

yellow starred   purple stalk

queen of the snow   ringed circles

torques   the mountain   slope

*

                  cherry to fawn

           walk left   ride right

      guest   the path continues   where

     a small bridge   can bear   eight tons

*

new growth   lights the conifer

garden on the roof

make   of your house   a forest

      [it's not magic   but there is   magic in it]

FRANCISCO MÁRQUEZ

Self-Portrait as the Falls

Didn't we rush? Smooth
    the stones?

Weren't the driftwoods
    home? Weren't horses

in blindfolds? Didn't their ears
    flit at the silence

in the wind switching?
    Weren't children

swimming, their mothers
    alone, retrievers

watching mist rise
    and gather?

What of our snake dreams?
    Trees uprooted

by rain? Storms
    veering

our coursing speed?
Remember

nights, used
by the moon,

her mirror? Or were we
witnesses?

BENJAMIN VOIGT

Olympic Valley

I never write about where I am. The present tense
rings hollow as a replica, as the start of a joke.

      Or am I simply afraid to write junk? I sit here,
      watch the empty gondolas climb up and come back.

You don't need me to see the mountain. It's there.
But how much of life do we never share with anyone?

      Or do we share too much? My legs are getting hot.
      The sun is sharp and white as a gnawed bone.

Anne Carson writes that written language requires us
to tune the world out to focus on these unmoving ants.

      The next pass is named for migrants whose wagon train
      mired in deep snows. Full of hunger, some ate others.

Sometimes I think I can't think on the page. It's blank
as a toothache. Sometimes I feel I don't have feelings.

      Chinese laborers bored tunnels for the railroads
      inches at a time, in pitch black, by hand and dynamite.

Now people come here to ski. Outside, cowbells ring
for the racers surfing down the slope for giant checks.

      The body a place the mind hides. The mind the body.
      Disembodiment a kind of embodiment, too.

Like a parasite, the Olympics always leaves their hosts
with ghost towns, plague villages, monuments to debt.

      Love or repetition do not make an idea true.
      But we do not necessarily love (or repeat) the truth.

What do I try to leave behind? More questions. My stiff neck.
Lack of perspective. Reckoning with what is. Whiteness.

      The resort as last resort. Or art as escape, as rest.
      A getaway. A retreat. Only the sea is further west.

II

Scrupulous Mercy:
Poems about Process

CORNELIUS EADY

You Don't Miss Your Water

At home, my mother wakes up and spends some of her day talking back to my father's empty chair.

In Florida, my sister experiences the occasional dream in which my father returns; they chat.

He's been dead and gone for a little over a year. How it would please me to hear his unrecorded voice again, now alive only in the minds of those who remember him.

If I could, if as in the old spiritual, I could actually get a direct phone link to the other side, I could call him up, tell him about this small prize of a week I've had teaching poetry at a ski resort a few miles from Lake Tahoe, imagination jackpot, brief paradise of letters.

How could I make him believe that I have gotten all of this, this modern apartment, this pond in front of my window, all from the writing of a few good lines of verse, my father, who distrusted anything he couldn't get his hands on?

Most likely, he would listen, then ask me, as he always did, just for safety's sake, if my wife still had her good paying job.

And I can't tell you why, but this afternoon, I wouldn't become hot and stuffy from his concern, think "old fool," and gripe back *of course I'm still teaching college. It's summer, you know?*

This afternoon, I miss his difficult waters. And when he'd ask, as he always would, *how're they treating you?* I'd love to answer back, *fine, daddy. They're paying me to write about your life.*

MAJOR JACKSON

Cries and Whispers

Each day I forget something, yet happy
I never forget to wake
to the bright corollas of summer
mornings. In the jury box of my bed,
I listen to the counterarguments
of finches and blue jays, cardinals and
the tufted titmice, and the sharp judgment
of the crow grow to sweet clamors.
In my neighborhood, someone like me
is sitting at a kitchen table taking down notes
between bites of granola and gentle sips
of oolong tea and recording the soap opera
in the trees. The pen is her large
antenna to the mysteries which come
in alternate currents of slapstick
and calamity. She writes away her nights
of emptiness and boredom. We'd be perfect
in a Bergman film, both of us entering into day
seeking the final appearance of things,
bumping around like this. A delivery truck
backs into a driveway. The streets
begin their excited breathing.

MATTHEW ZAPRUDER

What is the Naturalist Saying?

The chainsaws make it hard to tell.
Golden mantis? Let's go
smell a tree? That can't be right.
But I go and dutifully press
my two barreled pollen catcher
to the rough bark and say yes,
indeed, maple mixed with
a little cologne a jackass
dating your sister would wear.
Now he's into chipmunk tactics,
them watching each other
in the snow. Little black toenails.
Mutually assured nut destruction.
A mostly nocturnal mule's ear,
I drift in the useful wind.
With whatever the side
of the mountain that's winning
says I must agree. On sunny days
this I remember: I sure do love
my shadow more than I love
my mirror! The truth is I prefer
to be inside, silently visiting
a sick old hobbit irony
has not mastered. Some

jays are shy. I never knew!
Others will build
happily a nest in the spandrel
above the post office no one
enters anymore. Who even
writes letters? They are extinct,
like art you can't talk about
or Crypt Binaca. Now someone
from New Alabama is asking
a question exactly like she's
reading a manual just above
the naturalist's head. I can't hear
anything, the chainsaws
are coming closer, the hobbit
is saying goodbye to a boring life,
but at least he never shaved his feet.
In just a few hours it will be noon
and our shadows beneath us
into tiny circles smaller than a pin
will disappear, but we won't know,
we'll be so deep inside summer
talking we've finally been forgotten.

JUAN FELIPE HERRERA

Ritual Chant for the Strawberry Moon

Strawberry moon
     of the 4 quarters

     tahui tahui
     hello hello

I bring you these tiny leaves from the mountain
may they protect you
& you multiply in the rivers
may they take you
where there is no light
tahui tahui
so you may sweeten
the darkness
tahui tahui in the shape of a heart

PATRICIA SPEARS JONES

Lytic or how not to see The Strawberry Moon

The poet had too much to drink and so forgive her this lyric spelled lytic
Lytic are these stars in full array above the myriad evergreens oh how
They light the austere lawns of French estates but why French estates
In the *Sierra Nevadas*?   Eyes leap over peaks of these massive hills
Searching for clarity, but tongues sings gardens & the genesis of stories.

Consider the spirit of summer solstice in gratitude and perplexity.
The moon cannot be seen. The sun refuses to set in time enough
For the poet to see the large, red promised moon, the strawberry moon.
The poet is perplexed by this seemingly endless day light
The sun's refusal to surrender to night,

the mountains, these mountains are as drunk as the poet tonight—
the pollinating pine, the restless predators and their prey like
the moon moving where the moon moves—dipping her raiments in
        red dye.

Sun and moon and creatures hunting across mountains–then barking
        dogs in
SUVs populating small segments of wide parking lots. The wind
        chimes cheer.

Who will tell us our stories? Who will want to hear about
        drunken poets

The origin of "the strawberry moon"; how gardens blossom
        beneath these
Stars intensity. Luminous. Light. Clarity, Clare. Clara,
        oh poets' nimble
work these bones. Be done unto terra and air. Tales composed
        in patterns
of flight and tusk, gold and rubies, pine trees and mountain lions

Our songs start in exuberance and anxiety
Spirits work our blood and in the night's darkening air
Making bracelets of gem stones & animal bones
culled from blood oaths and rifle butts,
& tongues undone by drink and altitude

C.D. WRIGHT

Obscurity and Isolation

The left hand rests on the paper.

The hand has entered the frame just above the elbow
to reveal a half-rolled sleeve.

The other hand is in its service.

It holds a foggy glass up to a standing lamp.

Motel furniture. Motel paneling.

From the outside, what light slips through the blind
is grey, blue-grey.

The phone rings. The hand, conditioned to pick up,
hesitates, withdraws

before the ringing finally breaks off.

FRED MARCHANT

Fragments on the Last Night

What would slip by stands miraculously
under the window, hidden in a sentence,
a phrase, a ground fog lifting, or is it settling?

In a gravel wash, on a pale mossy stalk
of Great Mullein two goldfinches grip,
and the stalk sways like a wand.
The strip of shadow reminds me of breathing.

There are those who think the origin of poetry
is a deity. Others say it is only a part of the self
normally asleep. Some declare it is loss,
that mortal shale we all plummet toward.

Tonight I think it is more like breathing.

Like Whitman reciting poems to the surf,
aligning his rhythms, like breathing. Like a day
marked by love for yourself and at least one other,
which is just like breathing, only a little harder.

STEVE FUJIMURA

Walking Back from Workshop

No one's watching.
No one needs to watch.

LISA RAPPOPORT

Zeus, Athena, Sisyphus, Danae, and the Rest of the Players

Whole worlds are born each morning,
springing fully formed from the foreheads
of their creators. *Poesis* means making.
The poets have come to summer camp
to make something out of nothing
or out of everything, silk from the sow's
ears of daily life. Words are the currency, drab
and valueless, paper money with no gold
standard until joined as precisely as the natural
world aligns rock, quaking aspen, stream.
Would-be gods of the page, tyrannical and whimsical
by turns, we struggle with the task, pushing
letter against letter only to see meaning collapse,
beginning again, yearning for the day when
a poem greater than the sum of its parts comes forth
in a showering of bullion from above.

ROBERT LIPTON

What the Poet Does

It's not that he wants to be like Bukowski looking for his teeth
near the bar's toilet, vomiting in the Geraniums
but he likes his drink, not to assuage the fear of death
or the simple anxiety of flying, he likes the taste
doesn't have a problem with waking up to a headache
the size of a small Italian city, and isn't overly bothered
by being too drunk to find his way home on certain
warm nights when anyone would want to be out under the stars.

That one of those times was last night is neither here nor there
it was a little difficult to get to sleep wedged between the empty
aluminum beer barrels behind the ski lodge but not different
enough from lying awake in bed worrying about the placement
of commas in the broken sestina about his wife's miscarriage
it's not the miscarriage (her third), that was the problem
but the poetry implicit in these events requiring such a difficult form.

I understand this completely, the challenge is not the mourning
nor even the demands of some obscure piling on of lines
nor being soberly housed, in fact, he likes the taste and the stars
the roof of trees and the silence spread out around him
like a hushed audience readying him to begin.

Maw Shein Win

Dragonfly

the mountain I didn't climb
grilled cheese sandwiches fried in olive oil
loop of swallow
sun on my black hair as I walk uphill
out of breath cursing
binoculars on the table

stuffed terrier in a basket no eyes
empty organic red wine bottle
under a fit of stars
conversation with housemates about failed Mormons
and forgiveness and poets in Nicaragua
wooden box full of straw hats in corner

white butterfly circling a dead tomato plant on the balcony
two cardboard coasters that say *Berg-Brauerei-Zellerfeld*
money tree shifting leaning to the left.
cable car crammed with tourists climbing up peak
dry legs
desire to swim

my mother administering anesthesia
to a patient in a hospital
somewhere in Apple Valley
ten-pointed crystal hanging on wire
sending fissures of light across my arms
dragonfly knocking against a window

Suzanne Roberts

Advice for the Poet

Robert Hass says to be the accurate
reporter of your own consciousness—
A blond boy once told me, he could
eat a whole bush of blackberries.
I worry about the wrong things,
so I don't have to think about whether
or not it's a good idea to fuck
my ex-husband, or how I keep dreaming
about having a baby, my dog Riva
left babysitting. But I find myself in Paris,
in front of Van Gogh's Haystacks,
staring at all that doughy paint,
no matter how many blackberries.

Dean Young speaks of art, the automatic
life, and the confrontation of the aforementioned—
I don't think the hummingbird wants
to close her eyes and fly into walls,
bash her small head against the glass.
Oh, but if she did, what an exquisite corpse
she would make (Dada Dada Dada).
The parenthesis means move
elsewhere, then come back.
Either you love him or you don't.

Sharon Olds tells me to use the word squid jelly—

Cornelius Eady says if the little voice
says the poem sucks, put it away—
Oh little poem, into the drawer
you go. Bye-bye. Or step onto
that mean little voice with the sharp
edge of your heel, squoosh. Squid jelly.

Galway Kinnell says say the unsayable—
Fuck you, Poem.

GIOVANNI SINGLETON

MERYL NATCHEZ

Horse of Another Color

When it gets to the point that every flake of mica in the asphalt
looks like a poem, and each pothole looks like a metaphor,
it's time to pull back on the reins and calm that overheated horse.
Whoa, Nellie. Time to head for the stable,
chow down on some one-syllable words.

You've put in some hard tracking,
some fine sure-footed intelligence back on the trail,
and it's true that anything can be a poem
and you could be headed in an interesting direction
despite all evidence to the contrary,
but seems like it's time to give it a break.

And fresh clichés are always lined up at the starting gate,
skittery nags, ready to breeze down the field,
thundering hoof beats and all.
You don't want to mix with that crowd.

So it's time to call it a day, hang up your horseshoes,
put down that pen, and let those frantically chattering aspens
talk to themselves for awhile.

LAUREN K. ALLEYNE

Love in A♭

after Dean Young

Dean told us a story about Coltrane:
how one time in a recording, he hit
a wrong note—*a real clam*.
In the second take, he hit it again,
this time harder, longer.
The third time, it becomes the heart—
the sound all the other notes wrap themselves around,
a different understanding of the melody—
the song beneath the song: the stubborn beat
holding up the heaviness of flesh.

Amber Flora Thomas

In Retreat

I knew what it meant to stir,
to carry the riddle of tree bark away
from the trunk, to summon fold
upon fold in the press of flight

and push it all against the glass.
I had seen the tribulations before
and won love, like what my mother
held back from my father.

The dream shook in my throat,
its taste waking me. You were
scared I could write so easy, like
I'd slipped on a sheer gown

in the mountains at night. The moth
opened against your lamp light and
stared me down. You were asking
if I'd written the poem before.

I was distant. Then I crossed back
into myself with a laugh that cut
the evening down to frog sounds.
The moth preened its marble head,

the jewel in a tiara you didn't know
you wore. In the dream I traced
stone buttresses along a rocky trail
hiked in the morning. I was up there

when I wrote the poem. The moth
stirred behind you, and I disguised
more laughter with a shallow cough,
until I could write the poem again.

Troy Jollimore

The Poem You Will Not Live to Write

The poem you will not live to write—
the poem you would have written if only
you'd had one more month, one more day, one more hour—
is a killer. A no-holds-barred, balls-out
masterpiece, the one where you put it all
together, everything you learned, everything
you suffered, all the bits of being human
you spent your life gathering up. It's the poem
you have been waiting for all your life.

The poem you will not live to write—
the next poem you would have written after
the last poem you will write, which is,
it must be said, a perfectly decent,
unexceptionable, un-
exceptional poem, the sort of poem
you would have read in some magazine
or other had someone else been the author,
or made it through the first half, anyway,
and then maybe turned to the theater
reviews or the gossip column or else
just put the whole tiresome issue aside—
is, let's just admit it, a knockout.

There's no avoiding the fact.
The poem you will not live to write
is the one that would make the grocer's daughter
come back to you, it's the poem you'd wear
like a pair of expensive stolen shoes
to a wedding you weren't invited to,
it's the one that waits for you in the dark,
unseen in the underbrush just outside
the campfire's zone of protected light,
with nothing but an uninhibited passionate
kiss and your death on its mind.

JUDY HALEBSKY

The Sky of Wu

It's 4 a.m., the bar is closed, and Starbucks isn't open yet, so they keep talking, Li Bai at least. Du Fu is shuffling a deck of cards that is missing the ace of spades.

Play anyway, Li Bai says

Du Fu hesitates

Li Bai wants to meet Robert Hass, but I don't know his room number. And he's got a poem due tomorrow. *How about hot chocolate?* No dice.

Li Bai wants the party to start

    (I have not been displaced by the war, discomforted maybe)

Du Fu keeps shuffling

Let's write on a joker and make that an ace, I say

They scowl (novice)

    (I write letters to Joshua in Kandahar, he sends pictures back
        in uniform in a helicopter, tan with sunglasses, smiling)

Du Fu is smoking an e-cigarette. Li Bai is laughing at him. They want to meet Charles Wright but I don't have his number.

The night is already over. There's nothing that's going to start except the nature walk and then workshop.

We don't write the poems together, I explain, *we just talk about them*

Li Bai rolls his eyes

America, he says, *it's worse than I thought*

Brian Cochran

Egrets, Regrets

To look at Gogol's overcoat and see how the coat itself becomes the
main character in the tale, the way the poor clerk disappears beneath
the weights of value—social, personal, survival—invested in a thing, is
to see form. Not as shape or outline, but a kind of immanence. The way
feelings that are formless seek to attach to people dreams words theories
acts to exist in a material word that form lies trapped in.

No doubt my poetry errs, wrote Hopkins, *but as air....*

Air and err and air and err. A kind of sonic opening.

My regrets bend back their long necks to pick at the scapulars.

In the Marxist reading of Bartleby, the lawyer's indifference becomes the
main character in the tale. This feels like an allegory of form. In air.

To speak of the parable in parabola is to sing a little. Which isn't on the
agenda today.

Gogol's mistranslated overcoat is really the cloak of social concerns.

How difficult to put something out there.

Yamini Pathak

I Fail Again to Stay Up & Finish My Poem

I like to wake in strange places with
a lightening behind the eyelids, a dissolution
of dreams & darkness like cream
rubbed in slow circles on thirsty skin

On a forest retreat in Chichen-Itza, a stroll away
from blood-thirsty pyramids, that first human
striving for stars & science: it was the fuss of birds
old as archaeopteryx in canopied trees that
called first my ears into wakefulness

Perhaps, it was the sureness of iguanas, cold blood
warming like slow-cooked porridge under the solstice

Here in the patience of the mountains the moon is
faded like paper slipped into a bowl of water
Seven mornings I have woken in the mauve
& ridden the tides of breath until I found
myself on the shores of a poem

III

After Surfacing:
Poems Produced by the
Process in the Place

GALWAY KINNELL

Exeunt the Frogs

Though you yourself may not sing for long,

sing anyway.

        —Old-Frog saying

A frog smiles until its time is up.
Its mouth opens like the top of a Steinway,
its bass voice rivals that instrument
in volume and power.
Many creatures, including us,
when long bottled up, like to let go.
At evening, the lekking of a bullfrog
releases for this particular locality
the repressed feelings of the day.
More rhythmic, less counted-out, than poetry,
more piercing and more strangely seeming to be
the true pure voice of everything; that is, they cry
them with a peculiar calm wholeheartedness.

Before long we could be deprived of their voices
which have sung us earth's vespers continuously
from soon after our idea of the beginning.
Last night we thought the frogs sounded doleful.
More likely we were just out of sorts ourselves.

In the call of the gopher frog
we can imagine we hear the chant of a shaman
back from his year of living among frogs.

Sorrow booms in a frog's resonating chambers
stirring alarm in the bugs, slugs and woodlice
who wait with diminished hope in its digesting chamber.

An old lichenous stone sits by the pond's edge.
Without warning it propels itself through the air
and, on landing, reveals itself as a frog. At a frog
jumping contest I saw the winning frog
leap fifteen and a half feet. After a smooth landing
he sat a long time—like a Buddhist, or a car
out of gas left out on a lonely roadside.

Sometimes I wonder about a bullfrog's
several lives, a situation that is
not altogether unusual among
the critters, except that in the bullfrog's case,
the male is completely chaste
—one might have guessed it, given that bullfrogs
have the tragically stringy lips of the people
we pass in the street who have lost interest in kissing—
and do not copulate but merely fertilize
the female's eggs as she squeezes them out.

I have heard of frogs dying off
for a long time, perhaps since my childhood.
Is there an equivalent of a psychic seam

between land-creature and water-creature
that is riddled with leaks?
Is the skin of the frog
too porous to seal out toxic leach?
Do frogs simply give up trying
to adapt to two degraded habitats?

Born into a brew of cadmium and mercury,
they hop up and flee across a land of selenium and arsenic
under cover of their fixed smiles,
with floppy feet, and an extra or missing toe,
on endocrine disruptors. Why else
but that they know we are moving toward night.
During each hop, they scan for evidence
it is true: "Exeunt frogs exit omnes."

RITA DOVE

Sunday

Their father was a hunting man.
Each spring the Easter rabbit sprung open
above the bathroom sink, drip slowed
by the split pink pods of its ears
to an intravenous trickle.
There was the occasional deer,
though he had no particular taste
for venison—too stringy, he said,
but made Mother smoke it up just in case,
all four haunches and the ribs.

Summer always ended with a catfish,
large as a grown man's thigh
severed at the hip, thrashing
in a tin washtub: a mean fish, a fish
who knew the world was to be endured
between the mud and the shining hook.

He avoided easy quarry: possum
and squirrel, complacent carp.
He wouldn't be caught dead
bagging coon; coon, he said,
was fickle meat—tasted like
chicken one night, the next like

poor man's lobster. He'd never admit
being reduced to eating coon,
to be called out of his name
and into that cartoon.

It's not surprising they could eat the mess
he made of their playground: They watched
the October hog gutted with grim fury,
a kind of love gone wrong, but oh
they adored each whiskery hock, each
ham slice brushed subterranean green.

They were eating his misery
like bad medicine meant to help them
grow. They would have done anything
not to see his hand jerk like that,
his belt hissing through the loops and around
that fist working inside the coils
like an animal gnawing, an animal
who knows freedom's worth anything
you need to leave behind to get to it—
even your own flesh and blood.

TOI DERRICOTTE

Not Forgotten

I love the way the black ants use their dead.
They carry them off like warriors on their steel
backs. They spend hours struggling, lifting,
dragging (it is not grisly as it would be for us,
to carry them back to be eaten),
so that every part will be of service. I think of
my husband at his father's grave—
the grass had closed
over the headstone, and the name had disappeared. He took out
his pocket knife and cut the grass away, he swept it
with his handkerchief to make it clear. "Is this the way
we'll be forgotten?" And he bent down over the grave and wept.

YUSEF KOMUNYAKAA

Anodyne

I love how it swells
into a temple where it is
held prisoner, where the god
of blame resides. I love
slopes & peaks, the secret
paths that make me selfish.
I love my crooked feet
shaped by vanity & work
shoes made to outlast
belief. The hardness
coupling milk it can't
fashion. I love the lips,
salt & honeycomb on the tongue.
The hair holding off rain
& snow. The white moons
on my fingernails. I love
how everything begs
blood into song & prayer
inside an egg. A ghost
hums through my bones
like Pan's midnight flute
shaping internal laws
beside a troubled river.
I love this body

made to weather the storm
in the brain, raised
out of the deep smell
of fish & water hyacinth,
out of rapture & the first
regret. I love my big hands.
I love it clear down to the soft
quick motor of each breath,
the liver's ten kinds of desire
& the kidney's lust for sugar.
This skin, this sac of dung
& joy, this spleen floating
like a compass needle inside
nighttime, always divining
West Africa's dusty horizon.
I love the birthmark
posed like a fighting cock
on my right shoulder blade.
I love this body, this
solo & ragtime jubilee
behind the left nipple,
because I know I was born
to wear out at least
one hundred angels.

CLEOPATRA MATHIS

After Persephone

Heaven got sweeter, its paperweight curve
star-crazy at its purple center.
She'd found a god, a weapon in the works.
Something I hadn't noticed in the field
fought out of the layers and took her.
I tore away the land's every color,
withered the smallest grasses. Every heartbeat
went blank, I dismantled the ticking.

They only say what I took, not what I gave:
roots and strong light, glory
in the single shoot, green currency
of the just-born. From the irredeemable,
the buried—this is how a self gets made.
Remember, that darkness contained the seed
sealed in the swollen red globe.
Hell had to pay.

LUCILLE CLIFTON

jasper   texas   1998

for j. byrd

i am a man's head hunched in the road.
i was chosen to speak by the members
of my body. the arm as it pulled away
pointed toward me, the hand opened once
and was gone.

why and why and why
should i call a white man brother?
who is the human in this place,
the thing that is dragged or the dragger?
what does my daughter say?

the sun is a blister overhead.
if i were alive i could not bear it.
the townsfolk sing we shall overcome
while hope bleeds slowly from my mouth
into the dirt that covers us all.
i am done with this dust. i am done.

DORIANNE LAUX

Ode to Gray

for Sharon Olds

Mourning dove. Goose. Cat bird. Butcher bird. Heron.
A child's plush stuffed rabbit. Buckets. Chains.

Silver. Slate. Steel. Thistle. Tin.
Old man. Old woman.
The new screen door.

A squadron of Mirage F-1's dog fighting
above ground-fog. Sprites. Smoke.
"Snapshot gray" circa 1952.

Foxes. Rats. Nails. Wolves. River stones. Whales.
Brains. Newspapers. The backs of dead hands.

The sky over the ocean just before the clouds
let down their rain.

Rain.

The sea just before the clouds
let down their nets of rain.

Angel fish. Hooks. Hummingbird nests. Battleships.
Teak wood. Seal whiskers. Silos. Railroad ties.

Mushrooms. Dray horses. Sage. Clay. Driftwood.
Crayfish in a stainless steel bowl.

The eyes of a certain girl.

Grain.

TOM SLEIGH

Space Station

My mother and I and the dog were floating
Weightless in the kitchen. Silverware
Hovered above the table. Napkins drifted
Just below the ceiling. The dead who had been crushed
By gravity were free to move about the room,
To take their place at supper, lift a fork, knife, spoon—
A spoon, knife, fork that, outside this moment's weightlessness,
Would have been immovable as mountains.

My mother and I and the dog were orbiting
In the void that follows after happiness
Of an intimate gesture: Her hand stroking the dog's head
And the dog looking up, expectant, into her eyes:
The beast gaze so direct and alienly concerned
To have its stare returned; the human gaze
That forgets, for a moment, that it sees
What it's seeing and simply, fervently, sees...

But only for a moment. Only for a moment were my mother
And the dog looking at each other not mother
Or dog but that look—I couldn't help but think,
If only I were a dog, or Mother was,
Then that intimate gesture, this happiness passing
Could last forever...such a hopeful, hopeless wish

I was wishing; I knew it and didn't know it
Just as my mother knew she was my mother

And didn't…and as for the dog, her large black pupils,
Fixed on my mother's faintly smiling face,
Seemed to contain a drop of the void
We were all suspended in; though only a dog
Who chews a ragged rawhide chew toy shaped
Into a bone, femur or cannonbone
Of the heavy body that we no longer labored
To lift against the miles-deep air pressing

Us to our chairs. The dog pricked her ears,
Sensing a dead one approaching. Crossing the kitchen,
My father was moving with the clumsy gestures
Of a man in a space suit—the strangeness of death
Moving among the living—though the world
Was floating with a lightness that made us
Feel we were phantoms: I don't know
If my mother saw him—he didn't look at her

When he too put his hand on the dog's head
And the dog turned its eyes from her stare to his…
And then the moment on its axis reversed,
The kitchen spun us the other way round
And pressed heavy hands down on our shoulders
So that my father sank into the carpet,
My mother rested her chin on her hand
And let her other hand slide off the dog's head,

Her knuckles bent in a kind of torment
Of moonscape erosion, ridging up into
Peaks giving way to seamed plains
With names like The Sea of Tranquility
    Though nothing but a metaphor for how
I saw her hand, her empty, still strong hand
Dangling all alone in the infinite space
Between the carpet and the neon-lit ceiling.

GERALD STERN

Steel Pier

I leaped through a ring of fire
I was white with red eyes
I never missed I loved you
in that metal tank + when
it was dark I wore white
flannel pants with a perfect
crease + went to hear Gene
Krupa for a dime I was
living in ecstasy then.

BRENDA HILLMAN

In a Senate Armed Services Hearing

From my position as a woman
    i could see
        the back of the General's head, the prickly
intimate hairs behind his ears,
        the visible rimless justice raining down
from the eagle on the national seal,
      the eagle's claw-held pack of arrows
      & its friends. A fly was making its for-sure-maybe-
algebra cloud in the Senate chamber; it fell to us
        to see how Senators
re-shuffled papers, the pity of
      the staples, to sense when someone coughed after
        the about-to-be-czar General said *I don't foresee a long
role for our troops*, there was a rose vibration in the rug.
      From its position on the table the fly
could then foresee
        the soon-to-be-smashed goddess as in
  Babylon. More perception had to be, began to be.
      Filaments rose from the carpet as the General spoke,
the Senators were stuck. What
        were they thinking sitting there
    as dutiful as lunch patrols
    in junior high. From my position as the fly
i could foresee as letters issued

from their mouths like *General I'd be interested*

to know, some of the letters regretted that.

Fibers in the carpet

crouched. From

the floor arose the sense

the goddess Ishtar had come down

to bring her astral light with a day-wrinkled plan. From my position

as a thought i thought she might. She might

come in to rain her tears

on Senator Bayh & Senator Clinton, on Senator Warner

in his papa tie & Senator Levin, on Senator Reed &

Senator Hill—rain tears into their water glasses, Ishtar

from Babylon they had not met

before they smashed her country now or never.

Then someone—Clinton i think it was

but it might have been Bayh—asked whether this confirmation *will*

give breathing space for the new

General to unoccupy (*how do the dead breathe, Senator,* from my position

as a fly) & i forget who asked what isn't even

in the same syntax of this

language i'm trying to make no progress in, asked

how the army would unoccupy, by north or south?

A voice beside my insect ear

said, these Senators all have their lives:

kids with stuff to do, folks with cancer, some

secret shame in a quotidian—

the thing in front always producing

panic,— just like yours, the voice went, just like your life.

i tried to think if this was true but was too weak from
             flying above this notebook to pity them. From my
                         position as a molecule i could foresee
twelve Senate water glasses, each bubble had an azure
         rim, the ovals on
the Senators' heads were just like them, the breath they used
when saying °°A °° for *American interests* made the A stand still,
                 it had a sunset clause.
    They tried to say °°°*Safety* °°° but the S withdrew,
the S went underground. Would not
be redeployed. Refused to spell. Till all the letters stopped
         in astral light, in dark love for their human ones—

EVIE SHOCKLEY

improper(ty) behavior

racial profiling: the idea that there's no legitimate reason for driving while black.
take sean bell: he got 50 bullets pumped into his car for driving while black.

homeownership is also improper behavior, in cambridge and beyond.
ask henry louis gates—arrested in his own home for thriving while black.

seemed like the obamas' celebratory fist-bump might derail his campaign.
now they know they should avoid things like high-fiving while black.

inner-city hoops are, of course, appropriate—unlike swimming in the suburbs.
the *creative steps day camp* kids were booted from a pool for diving while black.

even b-ball can fall out of bounds, if the finals pit you against a whiter team.
the rutgers women's players were slammed on the air for striving while black.

post-katrina new orleans is open to anyone with the money to rebuild—
except the 9th ward, which they're discouraged from reviving while black.

it's all about belonging: even now, who belongs where is often based on who
belonged to whom. i sometimes wonder how i get away with living while black.

Don Mee Choi

i would love to be a flower—esp if i get to see
the list and pick my flower
> (I'm particularly fond of country flowers)
>> —later, cd

(March 12, 2015, 4:11 PM PDT)

swaying hydrangeas
white hydrangeas
rose of sharon
azalea
forsythias
cherry blossoms
declassified flower
UPI flower
classified flowers
baby azalea
blue hydrangeas
merely peony
flower of all flowers

—love, dm

J. Michael Martinez

Prayer III

Lord, listen for the alarm
every summer   with blossoms

                pale terrors

                              thieve you under-skies;

Lord, you blossom for the alarm
every summer,   & sit to wilt

              to free one of one's

                          unchangeable immortality;

Lord, you listen every alarm
for the   blossoms with summer:

             striped in every mad

                        grey vague new earth;

Lord, blossoms listen for the summer,
every alarm   with you

                    to sing the candle you sing,
                        "Water renounce rebirth";

Lord, you listen   for the alarm
every summer   with blossoms

or so the tablet was sung,
graved beneath an undrowned dream.

FRANCISCO ARAGÓN

Hair

for M

after Andrés Montoya & Francisco X. Alarcón

I.

who conceived that ravine
       or
       the contour
       of those slopes

Torbay
       —washing
over
       him as he swims—

is trying to say
           don't let
               the barber
           shave
        below
his collar

2.

I love
breathing
him in

my fingers
raking
his chest

a cub
wanders
the forest

MÓNICA DE LA TORRE

Equivocal Valences

A noun, a silent one, despite the assertiveness of such parts
of speech. An IOU of sorts, from a person like a lama, not a llama,
ridding us of free radicals, figuratively, with his glowing orbs.
I nursed a decaf while he upped the ante, promising pie in the sky.
A woman named Margo explained that although holmium (Ho) plays
no biological role in humans, its salts quicken your metabolism.

"There's a dent in my car! It's no hot rod, but still," some guy nagged
as I was heading back on my bike. I'd either done damage or it
       was a scam.
I preferred not to spar, so produced an ashtray, since he was fuming.
He went on hectoring. I, a bit deferential for the sake of all of us,
and that of my radius, kept my unruffled mien (à la Alcott) and got away
            singing do re mi fa sol la siesta...

In the dream, there is an infant son, and I am elated, ardently motherly
despite the kids' yapping. Are they ever to end? Osmium (Os)
      is the densest
of natural elements, Margo says, now in the dream. Lucky for me,
I'll get a dose of instruction while I yak about my son. In medias res,
I can be such a spaz, I've forgotten the man's rant. I've got a companion
and have missed that my kid's got lice and might need an enema.
      I go on

ad-libbing and ask Rosa, who also happens to be Margo, if she too is bifid, snake-like. Osmium is the densest of natural elements. She utters repeated nos; our differences become salient. "Where's the trove of
documents I found?

Their relevance might be nominal, but still." She brays, laughing, "Nada; no sé nada. At least it's not roe," almost in slo-mo.

This is unrealism. Its dos and don'ts made corporeal. Take a step, face a gun. No one's haggling. With her IQ, I'd rise from the mat, steady my cam, record déjà vu, and arduously vet elements such as these.

GREGORY PARDLO

Metaphor

It means to transfer or carry, as a man might carry
his namesake in his arms or on shoulders cheering, "we
bad, uh-huh, we bad!" as my father did when he saw himself
in me. As I came of age, however, I thought my father was,
in the sense that means *to hamper or impede*,
an embarrassment, which is, as all language is
essentially, a metaphor. I. A. Richards says a metaphor
consists of a tenor and a vehicle. My father would
point out that he's using a metaphor
to define metaphors, a literalization, like
when Richards himself asks if a wooden leg is a metaphor
for a wooden leg. My dad, Gregory Pardlo, Sr.,
before he died, lost his leg to diabetes. Even though he
himself would be the only person to see it, he insisted that
the prosthesis match
his skin tone. This is the same guy who gave me
a Hot Wheels car for Christmas. A joke, see. He'd promised
me a car when I turned sixteen. It shimmers on my
desk now, a kitschy muse with shark's teeth decals behind
the wheel wells. Before he died, I told him I would have
preferred a Matchbox car packaged in an actual matchbox,
literalizing the figurative commingling of tenor and vehicle,
more metonym than metaphor, a pedigree, in other words.
He told me to get the stick out of my ass. Greg Pardlo
is dead. Long live Greg Pardlo.

MAURYA SIMON

The Miniaturist

for Kali Sanders

Her brush clinks in the glass—water blooms
milkily with a million particles of pigment

swirling like a cosmic ocean. Fine sable hairs
bleed themselves briefly, then they're lifted

again to their pointed task: to touch up
a polar night where the stars are as delicate

as mites, where indigo shadows pirouette
from pine tree to peasant, with his tiny lamp.

It's here, in such reduced visions, that proverbs
are born: a heart knows best the needle's prick,

or: earth's the queen of beds, or: silence hears
its own music. Seldom are hungers as transparent

as in the minutiae of the locust's smile,
or in the diatomic dance of air against flesh.

Objects materialize like crystals in her eye.
Ambitious electrons colonize her mind.

Aggrandizer of moments, the artist breathes out
shallow tufts of air, drying the moon's thumbprint.

She pauses until she becomes a still life. Surely,
there's a pond quietly lapping in her skull, that

she should see the world's burnished tokens as
vessels for carrying her further inward; that

she can make matter *matter* as deeply as spirit.
Her universe is vast—a thimbleful of tides.

ROBERT THOMAS

Into the Poplar Trees

There are no mailboxes on the side of the highway
at Loveland Pass, Colorado, shagged by snow.
The moon is so smooth in the twilight! Why did we stop
just here? The car idles as you walk away
into the poplar trees for no earthly
reason. I light a cigarette, for once in my life,
out of the crisp gold pack you've left on the dash
and watch the smoke smudge some flakes of snow
before they vanish. This blackstrap shit
tastes like God's exhaust if he were a diesel truck
accelerating past me on the road to Denver,
headlights filling my rearview mirror,
horn blaring, then fading to a whippoorwill
that vanishes in a ragged tuft of spruce, the ember's
hiss on my lips. I'm so tired as I pace
the ice crust on the tar that when it cracks
I start to shield myself from the stars.
There's nothing to lean on. Ann,
I want to be a white stone
in the snow so you will love me. I want to be
a white-antlered elk that's never sniffed
the heady, sour-mash smell of human skin
so you will come back. I want

to be the exposed white throat of winter

offering itself to the distant, shimmering

fangs of one of its own kind.

ALICE JONES

The Knot

The complex knot of the heart grew
      from those two cells

buried in a deep-sunken chamber
      of her body. Furrowed

wet layers dilate to surround the gilled
      creature who breathes

through her blood, swims in the amnion's
      salt sea, bound

to her by rope-like veins, uses her
      to ingest the world,

to take bread and air and sun
      to metabolize

and bring them in, the rich liquid
      food of dreams.

*

Change comes when the knobbed curl grows
    Skin. The vulnerable

knot of the heart takes up its own beat
    not keeping time

with hers, but a counterpoint—the first
    separation;

the safeness of one new wall in between,
    the terror—it won't

hold and you'll be one more morsel of meat
    inside her, digested

into her vast shape as your fragile form
    vanishes, as water

is sucked from your small cells to feed the huge
    ocean of her.

Scott Reid

Discourse on Life in the Hive

Bees are Black, with Gilt Surcingles—
Buccaneers of Buzz.

      —Emily Dickinson

Buccaneers of buzz
you fashion the sun
after your own image

*

If words are flowers
so succinct is your language
that these words wilt

*

Your internal fizz
transforms
the opium of sunlight

*

With your wardrobe of colors
in closets of clover
you line your hive with the wind

*

Before your wings taste
of morning air
you recite this code of honor:

      steal not another's clover
      lie not to the Shasta daisy
      love flowers with the bluest scent

    *

Fuzzy coat of arms
your glance says fire
when you dance your thistle dance

    *

Your glowing abdomen
settles disagreements
with darts

    *

Flying between creases of sun
royal jelly glands heavy
you imitate
the order of clover.

CHARLES HARPER WEBB

Vikings

Overran my boyhood dreams—fierce
Blond beards, slab-chests,
Biceps gripped by bronze bands,
Dragon ships which terrorized my ancestors,
Weak Britons who whined to Christ:

No match for Odin, and the hard hammer
Of Thor. While other kids clutched
Toy guns and grenades, I swung
My plastic war ax: immune to bullets,
Refusing to die. While they dreamed

Of rocketing through sunny skies,
I dreamed of fjords, their crags and storms
Matching my dark moods, my doubts
Of God, my rages and my ecstasies.
I snuck in twice to see *The Norseman*,

Wincing but bearing it as the Saxon king
Chopped off Prince Gunnar's right
Hand. I gloried in the sulking gods
And ravens and great trees, roots
Reaching underground to realms

Of dwarfs and trolls. I gloried in the runes
On shields, the long oar strokes
That sliced through ocean cold as steel.
I gloried in the Valkyries, bearing slain
Heroes to the mead halls of Valhalla

To feast and fight and fondle blonde
Beauties forever, while we sad
Methodists plucked harps and fluttered:
Sissies mommy had to dress
For Sunday school. The day before

Christmas vacation, when Danny Flynn
Called me "a fish-lipped fool,"
I grabbed a trashcan lid and slammed
It like a war shield in his face,
Then leapt over his blood and bawling

And—while teachers shrilled their whistles,
And Mr. Bean, the porky principal,
Scurried for his ax—thrust my sword-
Hand in my shirt and stalked out
Into the cruel winter of third grade.

CB FOLLETT

Venus of Willendorf

Though you can cup her in your palm
you could not hold her
if your hands were continents.
She is river beds
and the rolling of foothills.

I say to you, those are hips
to birth a world; like
wind-carved rock receives
the mountain gods and shouts.

She is thighs
and breasts flowing into them,
milk that pulls us into life, carries us
from the dark places of safety
into the dark places of light.

Feel her warm your hand,
the hot transfer of rock into bone.
Long wombed in Earth,
smoke and fire in the wolf night.

How did we turn from the pomegranate,

shed fullness

from our woman-bones,

strive for boy-thin hips, deny our thighs,

reduce our breasts, when all this time

she waited to be found?

SONDRA ZEIDENSTEIN

Buddha Thought

I am tired of writing about seductive father and icy mother and—what's
    the diagnosis I
want?—*borderline* sister
but I can't give up until I have wiggled free of the conditioning of my
    brain
warped from defending myself from the trauma of pining and neglect
trapping me in a world of delusion.
The great Way is not difficult. It only avoids picking and choosing.
The compulsion of conditioned behavior is hard to explain:
like a pitcher filled with water and the last eight echinops of the summer,
and how the invisible water lets you, for all the distracting reflections and
refractions of bright white light,
see in to the stems and out the other side.
If I can see behind my numbing mother, my treacherous father whose
    moist palm
I still feel around my small fist,
If I can, in this lifetime, see behind my fear of my skinny sister,
    uncondition myself
from running in disgust from her bloodsucking, then longing to be
    restored to it,
if I can keep at it in my poems,
I can rise above hopelessness,
I can move the world an iota toward salvation.

ALICE ANDERSON

Joy Ride

No More Joy for Teen

—*New Orleans Times Picayune* headline

You put the key in the slot and you turn, igniting the night air with
fumes, the Buick oiled black with twenty years of misuse on back roads

and bayous. No-see-ums spin and jerk in the columns of headlight, which
point straight to the interstate. You are fourteen, everything a possibility,

nothing for sure. For now it is midnight, the lunar eclipse, your fight-wearied
parents are fast asleep. Who knows how you know how to do it, how to

ease into drive, push on the gas, and go. But you do it, and black grace
hurtles you out: you're gone. The Buick rocks along, a humid room of

Juicy Fruit breath, brittle leather chirping like bed springs, slick green
dash light filming every surface of metal and glass and skin. The night

is cool, gulf breeze edging off tops of salt pine savannas, edging in to
velvety magnolia buds closed tight, waiting to bloom. You cross the

bridge at Lake Pontchartrain, the stone and white steel pulled taut across
flat water, see ghost fisherman along the pier, gathered around a fire

with all the people they loved once on this earth. You drive and know
the world can be made over in your mind, in an instant, made over slick

like sunset postcards sent from seedy motel lobbies. Over the glass dark
the Buick almost flies, ticking a song that sounds like liberty. The moon

backs into darkness, waning. You notice for the first time how much light
there is in darkness, everything shining—glint of quartz in the asphalt,

a sheerness in the canopy of trees, even the skin of passing motorists,
their faces grim or tired or singing, their teeth white, dazzling as wet

shells. Pale light of moss and mold, swamp water and alligator and every
slow-growing thing. You see light in the sunken ribs of a dead dog on

the sandy shoulder, a still black husk in impeccable repose, facing
away from the road wind, slick casement of fur, smear of blood luminous

underneath. Everything you care for is awake. Your brother tosses, yeasty
warm in his trim cot, glow-in-the-dark stars stuck like wishes on the roof

tiles. You drive. Cut south, pass boiled peanut stands in the shadow of slick
new hospitals, slip under the false neon blue of floating Biloxi casino

barges, crossing yet another bridge to Ocean Springs. You do not, as the
paper will report, stop to pick up friends. You slip through the austere jade

shimmer of Gautier strip malls. You do not, as the paper will report, smoke or drink or turn 360s on the lawn of First Baptist Church of Vancleave. All

you do is drive, pass the sandhill cranes of Pascagoula, shy in the marshes, prettier than swans. For just one moment it is dark: pure black night. You

drive. And even though you see in the horizon's coming dawn a faint splatter of blood, you turn around. Even though you see your father at

the table, shirtless, smoking Camels, you turn around. You hear the echoing ring of the metal princess phone as it strikes your skull. Your

body, like a gift, soars through the night, toward his rage. Your brother, dreaming, limbs perfect as new branches, sleeps, and so you turn around.

Head west now, toward home, all of it so fast, the oaks and the light and the bridges and trees, until finally, you pull into the yard, kill the engine,

dust settling behind you in tufts like a ball of gauze thrown, unfurling in the air, filthy and picturesque. The slider is lit up blue-white from the set,

the glass opaque and filmy in great swipes of dog nose and handprints in the shape of waiting. You see your father: he's waiting at the table when

you slip in, set down the keys he picks up and slashes into your face. You take in sharp breath and think: *nightair*. The sun turns from pink to

white, seeping into every corner of the paneled room, you taste salt in your mouth and think: *rough water on the gulf*. And when the bone of your arm splinters like old kindling stomped on in the yard, the sound is like

a word whispered: *luck*. When the phone cracks your skull you think:

freedom. You close your eyes and see darkness emerging before you

like a bridge. You're a breeze now, a shore line, an engine ticking

gently, night star, black dog, a bird they can't see.

You're a story in the paper: *No More Joy for Teen*.

You're fourteen, everything a possibility, nothing for sure.

SJOHNNA MCCRAY

How to Move

I cannot look at anything
      so black as my father's leg
            or used-to-be-leg below the knee,

now a stump. If a child's doll lost
      it's flexible hand, the surface
            underneath would be as round

as father's stump. I've touched it once.
      And my brother, who is five, is
            not afraid to touch the stump.

Men on the corner used to holler
      that dad was a high yellow nigger
            or if the sun had darkened him

and pulled the red to the surface of his skin,
      a red nigger. I am thinking of colors
            because the prosthesis comes in colors.

His first leg was the color of oatmeal,
      maybe the color of peaches. Khaki,
            yellow and pink: a simulated sunset.

I am thinking of technicians

    with photographs creating

        perfect shades of negroness

for limbless negroes, every negro

    matched to a swatch or chart with names

        like fingernail polish. When my brother

touches the stump, the stump

    that has shrunk and hardened to look

        like an oversized, uncircumcised penis,

when my brother takes the brown

    almost black debris of father's life

        into small hands that marvel

at catching spiders in jars, he is not afraid.

    When we discover death, flailing

        in the gravel driveway, he knows it

immediately, the dark grey body

    of the robin, the red and slightly pink

        shaggy belly. The fuzz of the robin's round belly

like the fuzz of new tennis balls.

    The robin is on its side with the right wing

        moving slowly, back and forth.

At the same time, the beak is opening

      and closing. There's hardly any sound, no song

            except the sound of short, jagged gasps. All

elements working in unison: wing

      moving back and forth, beak

            opening and closing, the rhythm inherent

in knowing and not knowing when anything

      is coming, but wanting to finish it, gracefully.

            Even while dying. But maybe grace

has nothing to do with it; maybe

      it's desire that pulls our limbs, the robin's

            wing on concrete, to fly even in the shadow

of a man and a boy, the boy with his eyes

      ready to ascend, out of his mind, celestial. Maybe

            the desire is to show us how to move.

When we are at home,

      he takes the stump in his arms

            holds on to it like a prize or an unexpected gift

            that father has given us.

CARRIE ALLEN MCCRAY

The Children's Virginia

Virginia wind says home.
Screech of the front porch swing.
The big oak in the front yard,
its swing and singing:
Oh, how I love to go up in the swing,
Up in the sky so high.

The seminary across the road in summer,
yelling through its empty halls.
The big back porch with the long table
for summer's meals.
Chickens clucking around,
pigs in their pens.

Sad-eyed cow, Mary.

The sound the Southern
flagged on Durmid Hill.
Under the table
Buster the collie
on somebody's feet.

Across the road, Mammy Joe's store
for saucer-sized sugar cookies after school.
White Mrs. Limbaugh's cold lemonade and
ginger snaps, sitting in her swing,
singing children's songs.
Her son Luther there.

The down-the-road shack
where the best friends lived.
Paper stuffed in cracks.
The pot-bellied stove and their mama.
Collard greens with crumbled cornbread,
buttermilk the children churn.

FORREST HAMER

Grace

This air is flooded with her. I am a boy again,
and my mother and I lie on wet grass, laughing. She startles,
turns to marigolds at my side, saying *beautiful,*
and I can see the red there is in them.

When she would fall into her thoughts, we'd look for what
distracted her from us.

My mother's gone again as suddenly as ever
and, seven months after the funeral,
I go dancing.
I am becoming grateful. Breathing, thinking, *marigolds.*

JULES MANN

The Way She Played

She used to call me from her bathtub and we'd talk about insecurities and art. The one time I was in her house I sat there and conjured up steamed beads of water sliding down the ceramic jars the picture frames the religious icons the magazines and books piled on the thin wooden board across the middle of the tub ... but I couldn't picture her in it. She moved her mouth a certain way right before the shutter clicked, pursing up her lips in less a smile than a glazed mental kiss. Sixties. She never moved out of it from the waist up. She seemed to find pine cones a marvel and applied lipstick before climbing out of bed. Not gazelle though well-boned and emphatic about her paranoias. She was good at gazing maybe that's what I was thinking in that way the neck gulps forward wanting to be adored until everyone does and then she never answers the telephone. I think mundanity frightens her. The way she played with a loose strand of hair everyone believed her because she always came from somewhere else before that. Only once I felt her entire body separate between talk and definition. She was underneath me, everybody's ear against the wall.

THETA PAVIS

Consumption

I want the last pork chop.

The meat my brothers and sisters
used to reach for—
our hands flying over the table
our beak voices rising
our backs to the red, paint-peeling chairs.

My mother rationed summer fruit
like a benediction,
One plum per person. One peach.

She made rules about juice—
placing plastic jugs in the fridge,
announcing when we could drink.

Alone at 30
I drank gallons of it.
Hearing her voice with
each morning swallow.

My mouth to the carton.
My head thrown back.

Food still looks like
something to steal and
I want the fat goose, fatter.

BETH KELLEY GILLOGLY

Debt

Fresh from medical school, my father arrived
at the accident to find his big sister
already dead, the top of her car shorn
off, her body covered on the stretcher.

On her desk, he found stubs
from the shoe repair, the cleaners,
pick up dates circled. No letters
to answer. All her bills paid.

My father (who is always
late, never pays on time,
the dining room table fills
with notices to disconnect)
wonders what might happen
if he were all paid up, if
he ever stopped owing.

ELIZABETH ROSNER

Instructions

Fill your suitcase with black. Tell your mother you're on the way.
And when she says, Are you coming to see me kick the bucket?
say, I'm coming to see you kick it across the room. Later,
when you remember the last time, when she said she would never
see you again, tell yourself there was no way to know.
She was the kind of person who said those things.

Fly. Think about nothing. Think about air pressure, wind,
the speed of clouds. Pray for timing. Pray for time.
And when you arrive, and they're all there waiting for you,
allow yourself one mistaken moment of relief that everything
is all right, otherwise they wouldn't all be there to meet you.
Then look at your father's crumpled face. Fall down.
They will all pick you up eventually. But for a while, just stay there
and let everyone else flow around you. They will know.

Forget the rest. Getting to the car, the hospital. And then:
seeing her. The room with a curtain and some chairs,
the temperature of the room. Try not to remember
this picture of her instead of all the others. It's not really the last one.
She is already gone and this is just her body, except this is the body
you've always known. The first one. Of course you have to touch her.
It's been hours, while you were flying. So. She is cold.
And not there. Somewhere, but not there.

Forget the rest. Back in the car, back to the house
where she should be greeting you. Think about nothing.
Stay up all night with your sister and let her tell you about it.
About the oxygen and the organ failure and the DNR,
about how Dad kept telling her you and your brother were on the way,
she had to wait. About how it was before you got there.
Forget the rest until the next day. Blur it. The room full of display coffins,
the cemetery plots on a map. Writing her obituary on the computer
in the office of the funeral home with its bright artificial light.

Lose all sense of time, of place. Put on the blouse your sister bought
because it's something you have to tear and can never mend.
Listen to the rabbi. For once he is saying things that matter.
The people washing her body have asked her to forgive them
for any indignity they might cause. And inside the coffin, that plain
pine box, there are handfuls of dirt from Israel. Listen to the rabbi.
When he says it's time to tear your clothes, hold onto your brother
            and sister.
Hold on. The tear is on the side over your heart, he says.
Feel the fabric resist a little before it gives.

In the room with all the people, read what you've written for her,
and then lose the pages somewhere on the way to the cemetery.

Maybe she has taken them with her. She always loved your words,
especially when they were about her. Let them go. Follow the box,
and everyone else will follow you. Wear your mother's fur coat.
You are the only one it fits. Remember how cold it is,
and how the coat is so warm. Remember how the frozen leaves sound
under your feet. Notice that the hole in the ground looks exactly
like it's supposed to, roots and stones along the edges.

Listen to the rabbi again. Chant the prayer, the one you will be saying
over and over for the rest of your life. Take the shovel in your hands and
turn its back to the mound so that you're reluctantly using it,
so that it becomes a tool of your sorrow. Let the earth fall away.
This is the most righteous kindness. The one that can never be repaid.

ELIZABETH SULLIVAN

Inventory

On the underside of your rib, a puckered dark pink
nub of skin—another nipple.

Once this mark was searched for on suspected witches.
It was the devil's place for getting nursed.

They guessed that what he wanted was human milk.
The suckling bliss, the food. The membrane skin so almost-broken.

You carry this tiny badge, this changeling freckle,
because you are a savage man meant for a more virtuous world.

And I like to think it is not a botch of creation but
a little rose meant for a future that will grow

milk in the male body.

Johnny Kovatch

Letter #9

There will come a time when I walk this field
alone, when those who carried me are no more

than thoughts thread like jays through rows of flax.
There was a scene in my head:

jumping from a raft in a lake—shades of blue the body
entered as it unsheathed from the air.

It could have been a sign we don't go whole,
that a part goes first to deter fear as the rest

follows. And memory? A screen door,
snapping back from the boy who ran

into night chasing after firefly. Who knows why
the lake suspended me in nothingness

where, after surfacing, I thought that wasn't so bad,
it even felt right, and that's why I'm so afraid.

THANDIWE SHIPHRAH

But to Lose Themselves in It

This man and woman are strongly attracted to one another.
Imagine that you can see inside their heads.

What is
is physically before them.
The matter of days and a silence we can't decipher.

So how will they connect what has gone before?

Hair kept falling away from his fingers.
His were eyes she couldn't see into—a kind of blindness,
"what if."

Look at the way he keeps looking at her.
What will happen next?

The process of recollection?
His earliest memory selecting itself?

Wonder is all she can do.

He felt like "yes" to her,
and "isn't this what you wanted?"
Or is it beauty he's trying to understand,
the way we're trying to understand their hesitance?

Or are they going forward?
Were it to happen it would need to happen quickly.

It would have to be held firmly in place,
a letting so tightly fixed as to render choosing.

Impossible is what they were used to.

"Here" is what was meant to be perceived,
to be tested and then examined.

What may yet prove correct?

Did he ever turn away? Was she abandoned?
Was he?
What remains to be seen?

And what about what we call for?
(The question so loyal, so intensely there).

Look there. Beneath their ideas.

No, further.

Beneath the idea of "them."

Yes, there. The language they were after.

Isn't that what we're always asking?

How faithful? How steady the ebb and flow?

LOIS ROSEN

Strudel

Strudel making is not a picnic. So better you should find a nice bakery and buy your strudel there.

The Chinese Kosher Cook Book
Ruth and Bob Grossman

Give me a nice rye bread well-browned, a nice piece of strudel. A nice corned beef, a nice pastrami, a nice tongue. That's not a nice way to talk. Have nice Jewish friends. Marry a nice Jewish boy. Be nice to me I might die soon. Nice and easy. Play nice. That's a nice way to treat your parents. You're not nice. Nice going. Nice try. Nice as pie. You'll sleep in a nice warm bed. Some nice present you brought me. How nice of you: say it no matter what the gift. If you can't say anything nice, don't say anything. Some nice mouth you have. Get a nice job: be a teacher with a nice salary, nice benefits, a nice pension, nice summers. Some nice weather we're having. This is the nicest thing anyone's ever done for me. A nice gesture. Say it nicely. Make nice. Be nice to me I might die soon. Did you forget? Another nice mess. Nice way to talk to us. Some nice daughter you turned out to be. Nice sermon. Nice music. Nice eulogy. Nice funeral. So nice of you to come. So nice of you to invite me. So nice of you to remember. Nice knowing you. Have a nice day, a nice trip, a nice life. Nice as can be. Nice and fattening. Nice and juicy. Nice and hot.

Danusha Laméris

Eve, After

Did she know
there was more to life
than lions licking the furred
ears of lambs,
fruit trees dropping
their fat bounty,
the years droning on
without argument?

Too much quiet
is never a good sign.
Isn't there always
something itching
beneath the surface?

But what could she say?
The larder was full
and they were beautiful,
their bodies new
as the day they were made.

Each morning the same
flowers broke through
the rich soil, the birds sang,
again, in perfect pitch.

It was only at night,
when they lay together in the dark
that it was almost palpable—
the vague sadness, unnamed.

Foolishness, betrayal—
call it what you will. What a relief
to feel the weight
fall into her palm. And after,
not to pretend anymore
that the terrible calm
was Paradise.

BRANDON CESMAT

The Long Pass

On the football field, some fight, others run away
after the long pass. For all the shoulder pads' clatter and
helmets' crack, football is less culturalistic Darwinism than
a complicated game of catch.

People who love me have always done so in spite of my desire
to hit and shove with or without pads, on grass or sand or mud
as long as the light holds,
                                    the light necessary not to illuminate
the lineman who could dance like a dozen sumo wrestlers in the dark.
We light stadiums because football is a game of sky.

When I played tight-end—a halfway-house position for lapsed pacifists—
most of the game I would swing my forearms, throw my shoulders,
and drive my legs into the man across from me.
I was yell, muscle, grunt and rumble.

But for a few plays, I would release from the line and run downfield,
trying to put distance between myself and everyone. It felt good to be
        alone and
hope the ball would fall over my shoulder, into my hands, as soft
as I could make them, hold on tightly and run as far as possible.

For all the yelling, I learned to listen for football's quiet.
The long pass flies silently, is no "bomb" unless dropped.

The long pass is a prayer with answers.

After the ball's snap,
the charge of the line, and
calls to put the quarterback in a sack,
the spinning oblong sphere brings a hush.
So much can go wrong between
your hands and mine.

The linemen lean back from one another as the ball reaches the apex,
and even drunks in the bleachers quiet as the ball starts to drop
into that moment when we all lift our eyes and together take a breath.

Renato Rosaldo

Ode to My Shoes

Shoes, you wait every morning
on the floor, in a row, to be filled.
The shoehorn slides my feet
between your heels and your laces.
Embraced by your firm fidelity,
I walk you down the street.
My gait shapes you, wears you
more on the heel than the toe,
more the outer than the inner edge.
You absorb dank odors of decay,
the indentations of my thickening nails.
You shield my feet as I walk 15th Street
to the Westside Market and scrape you
on the sidewalk as I try to keep an even keel,
for I'm an aging vessel that yaws to the right.
A man asking for coins lowers his paper cup,
Have a nice day, hope you feel better, he says.
From here, shoes, we might simply decline.
You could become scuffed like me, as we grow old,
more fragile, perhaps, one day, immobile.

J. O'Nym

Blue in the Face

When I was a child, I could hold my breath for such a long time,
I imagined I could dive for pearls.

                    Back then, I tortured strangers
at the lake—I'd pick some unfortunate woman and do the dead man's float
next to her. I kept my eyes open, allowed time to drift by, watched her feet
and legs become concerned, then panicked—until she plucked me right out
of the water to look into my face.

                    It never worked with a man. I might float
there for an hour, bumping up against him like a dinghy tied to the dock,
but he could not bring himself to see me.

                    I held my breath once, from 1959 until 1975.
My father, noticing for the first time that there was someone else in the room,
put down his glass. It was a world record of sorts—not quite
irritating enough to transform a grain of sand, but almost.

Yiskah Rosenfeld

Yehi Or (and There Was Light)

At 3 am I went in search of the lesser light that rules the night

　　　　　　　　　　　　　　　　according to the Bible,

and the second brightest light in the night sky according to USA Today.

I put on a T-shirt, glasses, and shoes and believed myself

　　　　　　　　　　　　　　　the Invisible Man,

nothing more than the things themselves with night unimpeded between.

But when I stealthed from the house a flurry of lights popped up:

first the lamp I'd turned on in my bedroom window,

revealing a strange, superfluous scene

in which no one was sleeping in the bed.

Then one after another like a movie jailbreak, bang, bang, bang.

The porch, the yard, the stairs—lit, lit, lit.

Lights chased me down the black road and, as in a fairytale,

tricked me past the gates of safety.

There in the dark pool of road,

I felt the covert strength and height of my legs.

The brilliant half-moon punched a light in the sky not lesser than—
the Bible was wrong—but equal to the sun, just turned in on itself.

And in a web of sticky, numberless stars, Mars—USA Today
got it right—was one bright orange piercing, closer than it's been

for 50,000 years.

So there we were.
Forming some new constellation:

Half-moon   Mars

        the empty bedroom

                                a woman   6 lit steps.

None of us were close enough.

Did other constellations feel this?
Allied but estranged?

The handle of Ursa Major
longing to taste the milky soup in the bowl,

Orion's hand itching
for the distant grip of his sword?

I wanted to know the moon's pale, graveled wholeness,
to flesh Mars out to dry red riverbeds of dust.

Instead I followed the 6 lit steps like luminous crumbs
across the lit yard, into the house, back

to the bright, abandoned room.
There I showed the moon and Mars my lesser light.

DEVI S. LASKAR

The All-Saints, GA., Overeaters Support Group (meeting #18)

First we talk about watermelons—
a modern, American reference
to family picnics, seed-spitting contests,
abating a thirst for summer love
by eating weightless pink flesh.

Then our study of the Greek myths
seeps through our tongues as pomegranates
are hurled onto our invisible
table, pungent olives, golden
apples, blood oranges, Medea.

Someone comments on sorrow
as an appetite suppressant—
death provokes fasting, in some cases
a strict diet of bitter remembrance
until the taste for life returns.

Others blurt out hors d'oeuvres stories
at the theatre, cocktail parties, movies.
And at weddings, how the cake is too sweet,
the toasting champagne always falls flat
by the time the waiter reaches their glasses.

We discuss the reluctant meals we swallow
when there is no money leftover after rent:
white bread that's three days old, noodles,
peanut butter without the jelly,
lentil soups with rice, bags of popcorn.

No one mentions why we come here,
the way we slide into our chairs, batter
stealing home, without notice, without
admitting that we want to soufflé
our bodies from landfills to temples.

We laugh at the staple of fairy tales:
apples poisoned by jealousy,
gingerbread houses, cooked goose,
blackbird pies, cooling porridge, stone
soup, beanstalks that lead to giant feasts.

Then someone mumbles a fable about
the seven sins but I am too far
away to hear it, a joke that
I don't understand because I can't
get past gluttony and avarice.

Finally, a discourse on Vegas:
the incandescent dramas, all night
slots and sex, currency exchange
and love, how breakfast is served
at these twenty-four hour buffets.

It's about choice, I say. The use of buffet
is to speak of selection; the hierarchy
of egg dishes, for example:
how Benedict is better than poached,
the sauce enhancing the runny yolk.

No, a voice calls out from the circle:
Buffet is all-you-can-eat,
it's tasting a lot of everything,
eating it all. Freedom and acceptance.
It's taking the whole world into your heart.

The hour is up and I am hungry.

SHOLEH WOLPÉ

The Village Well

We were children, curious. Something splashed
in the belly of the well and you took my hand, descended
into the mouth opened wide,
step by concrete step down its dark spiral throat.

The creature that unhinged the damp stillness
of that well was not a man, not an animal—
just the silhouette of something vast…
I thought it was God, you thought it was a djinn,
and then you with fear did not think at all, running back up
breathless, the chill of the well at your heels.

That night you didn't wait for his leg to accidently
rub against yours, or his hand to accidentally brush
your thigh as it always did, away from eyes that never
blinked. Instead, you reached for his knee, the flesh and bone
of this gray man who pretended to be daddy's friend. Beneath
the table laden with almond rice our mother had lovingly cooked,
the saffron-stewed lamb, the chicken smothered in herbs…
you squeezed,
squeezed so hard his eyes turned your direction and melted
into a watery scream like the one still rising in the throat of that well.

MARY AUSTIN SPEAKER

The Population of Philadelphia Wants Their Eagles Back

Over there, someone says, pointing up the hill,
which means either beyond the hill or somewhere

on its forested face. It's a steep hill, full of caves
and hermitages, but placing your arms behind your back

helps with the climb, unless you're carrying a giant nest.
It's hard enough to find an eagle, let alone begin

the repopulation process. David Ignatow says the solution
is to be happy with slaughter, but he believed in innocence.

When confronting the unfaithful lover, don't bother
weighing each word, but it may be necessary

to get onstage. If you make it that far, if jokes don't work,
try lulling the crowd by explaining the solitude

of eagles, their terrible grace, imperturbable feathers,
lack of camouflage, and how they will never be satisfied

with artificial residences any more than human beings
thrive in housing projects. *We must always be aware of the worst*

possibilities, says the eagle, shredding your couch
into tufts of softness, *and learn how to rise on the current.*

When eagles are born they are entirely white
except for their beaks, which are black. The juvenile eagle

is a mottled brown. A baby desert eagle is a kind of gun.
In Philadelphia, says Jane Jacobs, the sidewalks are so wide

the city takes care of itself, but she believed in innocence.
Possession of an eagle feather or other body part

is a felony with a fine of up to $250,000 or imprisonment
except by enrolled members of federally recognized Native American
        tribes,

who are imprisoned at four times the rate of whites.
Given something of value, we become marvelous keepers.

The eagle's beak is his mercy. He uses his sharpest parts
to spare the animal pain, and when he flies, he hardly moves at all.

KEETJE KUIPERS

The Undeniable Desire for Physical Contact among Boys of a Certain Age

They can't keep their hands off each other, irresistible,
the hard, narrow barbs of their hips, the feet
long, having already outgrown the body
in a fit of physical genius. New muscles are forming
like buds every night in the seams of their flesh
'til they wake to a flower that still lacks a certain
metronome for the glory of its bloom. These boys
scoff at the idea of desire, punish those who succumb
to its hum, but the thin beams of their fingers fall
in searchlights on flanks and sweat-filigreed brows,
they brush lips to an ear and out tumbles breath
they know they can't hold. Every nimbus of laughter
encircles an incomplete touch, a hand on a knee, a tongue
in the air, the divining rod wending one from the other.

CHRISTINE HEMP

Olive Leaves Trembled When They Heard the Harp. Grasses Hissed with Pleasure.

(Eurydice)

Thirsty for his notes, they loved him, too. But after the wedding,
the wine and figs, the merging of our flesh, when he had to show me

to the forests and fields, I begged him not to take me too far
into the glade. Marriage, after all, was new.

I wanted to go home. My beloved paused, the wind
breathed in. All of nature waited for the braided chord. That's when I

ran across the meadow, tipsy and confused, just as dusk
had slithered in the shade. My bare feet, unused to such

terrain, throbbed. I thought I knew the way, but stumbled
and was lost. My dress hem ripped, and stars began their chatter.

Fast-forward to the grave and what I felt when I went under,
viper's poison turning into heady brew. I didn't want to come back.

It isn't what he told you: I was no hostage. The darkness gathered
and released me. With each step down to the Styx, confusion waned—

I no longer worried that I'd lose him to the fawning crowds
whose devotion to his art I could not match. I wouldn't have to

bear those taut adagios, each pluck of the string making me
(just like those trees) ache and bend for more, a slave to utter harmony.

ARLENE BIALA

ala moana beach park, 1944

for jane del rosario

her hands are sticky. her fingertips trickle juice.
strands from mango seed are stuck between her teeth
that toil to scrape the seed clean.

she looks down at her legs, darkened to lava rocks.
she knows her mom will beat her when she gets home.
eyes closed, the smell of rain coming over the ko'olaus.

she sucks on the seed again. this is her favorite part:
after school, after running down the beach,
clothes, backpack, slippahs shed to sand,

sitting in knee-deep water, waikiki chaos behind her.
this is where she savors the scavenger hunt,
ripe prize of the softened globe she cups in her hand.

bite down to peel, slurp slivers of fruit
down her throat, she flings the strips of skin
to watch them float away like lost paddle boats.

beyond the reef, she whispers, and wonders
how far she can swim—maybe out to the point
where the surfers shout and slide, drop from the lip

of a twenty-foot wave, or how far she can fly
soaring over the cemetery in punchbowl crater.
hello grandma sakamoto, aloha papa john

but it's time for her to go, to circle back makai.[1]
she waits for a sign, smells burnt stalks of cane,
she doesn't hear the hum of fighter planes slipping by.

---

1. makai: toward the sea

CHANDA FELDMAN

Approaching the Fields

We're so close that we can't not stop—fields,
late fall, days after the killing frost, and the cotton

ready for harvesting. The bolls shocked open—
unspool ripe cotton on the wind until we walk

into a blizzard of it. My mother wishing
her mother and aunts and uncles could look up

from the rows ahead at her and her sister,
picking. They called my mother *Coo* for slim-

beaked fingers pinching cotton from the boll
without getting pricked on the plant briars. Now,

the process is machined, spindle pickers reaping
eight rows at once, the bales, like loaves

of plenty, wait for a trip to the gins at the field's
ends. My mother's been trying to tell me

about where she's been. My mother, who crossed
the threshold of the afterlife, who died

her three minutes before her heartbeat was revived,
who came back with a sense that there was no

heaven's gate on the other side, not even
something like night, like quiet, that if she was

absorbed into anything, she was lost to its workings.

KEITH EKISS

Pima Road Notebook

Forget what I said about the snakes.

It isn't all holy.

Call me the child who wouldn't burn the ant nest.

The scorpion quivered on my brother's shoulder.

I went to school and came home from school.

The hunchback boy fed pink-eyed rabbits.

Kissing Tomi Kaye by the horse corral,

I opened my eye to see the fine hair above her lip.

One flat stretch of road leading on toward the horizon.

I bb'd the quail.

Steven said his father died, we were pissing

at the urinal, he told me it was okay, he believed in Jesus.

What they said about Loper, his father dealt coke.

Fathers just leave—isn't that what fathers do?

Coyotes at dusk crossed the 17th green.

I fed the dog and picked up shit.

Followed my mother downtown to the bank.

Paper bag bottles, pimps and pumps.

My apology—too late for the blind boy.

Bloodied Ty Liddy's nose beneath the bridge.

Two snakes in a pit? *Bad luck*, says a Pima.

Spitting out sunflower seeds;

that drugged fatboy chanting my name.

The neighbor groomed horses; I never saw him ride.

Then he showed me where he hid the guns.

CHING-IN CHEN

Feeding the Water

a bop

River between us grows solid
monsters and red meat
compost sludge sneering
the rain I dream unending
water top layer oil and dark
bobbing heads

I'm waiting for that final moment
You'll say the words that I can't say

Each ghost owns her own birth story
but death belongs in the open
we burn firewood gold houses
sweet rind she billows
fat I am sick unyielding
haunt can't be chased out with
candlewick bribed with sweetback
pork the seal of red

I'm waiting for that final moment
You'll say the words that I can't say

But two ghosts in one house
unraveling spools of black thread hair
your still face spread against the pillow
maybe exiting dream
or smothering stars
against the airtight window

I'm waiting for that final moment
You'll say the words that I can't say

LEAH NAOMI GREEN

In Cleaning

the room where I want to rest,
I find my hands and am able

again to see you—
clear eyed where we left one another—

last year in the passenger's seat,
having woken after Colorado, which was beautiful

and which I did not wake you for,
wanting all the aspens,

all the golden, quaking aspens, and their silence
for myself.

LARRY RUTH

Willow

...dearest to me was the silver willow.

—Anna Akhmatova

(I) count every tree down and up the red gum street,
the eucalyptus butchered until forgetting its treeness
withers and dies, the planted replacement a weeping
willow, light green in July, long branching whiplike
wands, two neighborhood boys skateboard by, dare
the coach hounds three doors down, play lion tamer,
teasing, taunt them, tangle as the least of us prepare
for playground glory, blackberry bramble, bullyboy
bravado of checkered flags and fists, falls and skinned
knee silence, compassion is a badge for losers, see,
poison oak–plagued cushioned landings, those black
eye bruisers, kin to the stump, where a winding stair
rises, built by Tom and Tim, three stories high, seven
years' labor, father, son, time and the willow flowing

going

going

gone to light.

ANDREW KAUFMAN

They Killed Our President
Kigali City Prison, 2008

for Eugene Nikinahe

They killed our president. He is like our father.
I am trained by Interahamwe.
They kill our leader to get power
and force us from our country

We all belong then to Interahamwe.
Each one we kill—a collaborator.
Yes. They try to force us from our country.
No. I did no looting. I did no torture.

The men we killed? I said, *collaborators.*
We had only knife, stones, and machetes.
I told you, *No looting. No torture.*
We send for help when we find big families.

Only weapons—I said, *knife, spear, and machete.*
What I was thinking then? Nothing. Just the war.
And get help if we find large family.
The only one I killed—he was an invader.

I was thinking nothing then. Just the war.
I cut him. Twice. The throat. Yes—machete.
He was alone. The sergeant said an invader.
I was working the roadblock to keep security.

I cut his throat twice with the machete.
I saw many bodies in the river.
Orders were to *work roadblock*. For security—
My job then is to protect our sector.

I see countless bodies floating in river.
The number killed at roadblock? Maybe eighty
traitors. Our job was to guard our sector.
Some killed send children. To help our enemy.

Those I help kill at roadblock? Maybe sixty.
I do not want talk to you anymore.
I tell you they send children to help our enemy.
What reason you ask your questions for?

I don't want talk to you anymore.
In some houses we have to terminate babies.
What you asking your questions for!
Our group's orders come from ruling party.

I have no thoughts when they terminate babies—
enemies invading us to take power.
The orders come from ruling party.
I love our president. He was like our father.

ALIX ANNE SHAW

And After

Caught in the oak tree's wickering light, knee-deep,
without rescue, I have grown raw white as a mollusk. I can't bear

to hear music, no longer listen to the radio. In this town
there are toxic salt-flats, lemon trees, the smell of lanolin.

In the streets there are cathedrals, marble forms of saints. The saint
with a wasp in his mouth, saint with a rabbit

hedged beneath his arm. Behind the rabbit's eye, a coiled spring.
But my hands, a tattered ledger, offer only evidence

without imperative. I found a nest of bees inside the grill
and lit them each on fire, rubbed their soot and honey in my hair.

But there was no visitation, no vision
that could lend me back the day. The rabbit squirmed

from the stone grasp of the saint. *Already, friend*, I murmured, *I like you
more than is meet*. I will bring you blood and muslin, anoint your lips

with milk, tie you by the leg to the mulberry tree.
I will drop ink on your tongue to be sure you speak no ill

till the workmen come with leather on their hands. I know one
bit of magic: how to turn invisible in a room. The trick

is turning visible again. I will make a clipped beginning
but I say again I am no kind of bird. In this town there are roofs

of copper, angelica staves in the yard. In this language
the word for *lid* is the same as the word for *sky*.

Hillary Gravendyk

Botanica

Creature of occasion, remember where you have been, which leaves
have teeth, which leaves are shaped like a pair of lungs. The closed
landscape glitters. My name is *Acutifolius*: having sharp edges. Underside
of each frond like a powdery line of Braille. Air stuttering with leaves.
There's a night inside the night inside my chest. Forest air cool as a
plum's dark flesh. The hand goes black against the low green. I'm
Candicans: looking white or frosted. Or *Sylvaticus, Californicus.* In the
crowded wood, I see the several eyes go down. Black air folds around
low ferns. Asleep, I laid my hand on the tree until my skin turned to bark.

DAWN McGUIRE

Angelus Novus

There is an appointment between the generations of the past and that of our own.

For we have been expected upon this earth.

—Walter Benjamin

Walter Benjamin's slouching across
the Pyrenees again, carrying the lost manuscript.
A minute's rest after ten minute's climb;
he figures he can make it to the end.

The black case is heavy, the contents
wrapped in haste. Ten minutes
then a comma, then another ten, jackboots
right-lefting on the road just above.

Soon he will make it to Port Bou,
soak his fallen arches, address
the package to a friend, take
too much morphine for the pain.

It will be said that the manuscript
was never found, or that it never was.
But today lost quotes will be read
in People's Square

by a young woman with bad teeth.
She will lisp into the microphone.
She knows the State is on its way.
But the Friend is already in place,

hair blown back, jacket spread
over the wreck of the millennium,
counting off the intervals and rests.
For all that is ruptured

is repaired upon the page.
The passages are linked.
The port can be seen from here.

EMILY PÉREZ

Advice to My Younger Self: Fall

This is no father, man of sticks and splinters.
A kindling heart, unaware that each match will catch
its passions. Remember, it's never enough to banish

flint from the kingdom. A field mouse will reveal
the alternate route to the hideout, the spinning wheel's
spindle always arrives on the crone's cart.

And this is no mother, woman of bread crust
and broom dust. Consumed in mapping her shadow,
turns her back while dogs and rats roam the larder.

It's not that your songs don't amuse. It's not
that the tricks of your little bird hands do not please
or that you should search harder, run faster

from forest to field to hearth with your harvest
of seeds, extra mouthfuls for all, in your pockets. No.
If the pond swill ever stills to a glass fit for scrying

here's what it might show: In the hollow tree's hull,
blind, furless kits hiss, as the falcon describes its circles.
But in the room with no door, no one ever knocks or enters.

VALERIE WALLACE

Aubade

I don't need carp to jump from the lake
to know underneath swims its destruction

or see my mother's brain scan to know fear
resides in small actions

but I need to see slurry fog pull the sea into the valley,
before it leaves behind cars & starlings

& I needed to learn a lacewing can nibble itself out of the web
before the spider knows it's gone,

that it takes a long time,
to make yourself a tube of wing

& not often but sometimes, I need to open coriander husks
for the dusty seeds, their bright bite

& when I'm away, before my day ends,
I need your voice to tell me your day's story,

your voice that is aspen, sidewalk, bicycle, your name, my name.

Joan Baranow

Follow-Up Appointment

You'd think that inside the open incision
the tumor would declare itself
as obvious, a hard pit
darkish and persistent,
unwilling to let the flesh go,
but the surgeon explains that cancer
looks like healthy tissue,
that's why the marker with its metal hook
gets pushed in,
why she must excise widely
to keep the margins clean.
Similar, I suppose, to skirting
around a volatile dog
or how, just this afternoon, I kept
a good distance between me and the guy
dancing outside the gas station,
who asked, "How're you doing, Sweetheart?"
and I said, "Fine, thanks,"
and felt, actually, a little happy
even as I glanced quickly away,
my body still visibly female,
all of me as yet intact,
even my blonde-dyed hair.

BRENT CALDERWOOD

Abecedarius

Already they have decided what he is. He is a

Boy, barely twelve, but to them he is a

Cocksucker, a queer, a sissy.

Denying it only draws attention.

Each day they teach him a new word:

Faggot.

Gay.

Homo.

In the absence of actual proof, these might be idle

Jokes. Maybe the children are just

Kidding when they tell him what his

Lisp means, that he wants to

Marry a boy. He learns

Never to use words that start

Or end with "s."

Plurals are out of the question. Things are singular, or alone. He

Quits going outside at lunchtime. Kids throw

Rocks, scrawl words on his locker,

So he goes to the room marked BOYS at

Twelve each day, pretends to

Urinate, then stays in a stall till the bell rings at one.

Vaguely, he remembers a time before

When he could be here without seeing

X-rated drawings of himself on tiled walls. It was just a
Year ago. He would be here for a minute at the most,
Zip up his pants, then go back outside to play.

JOSEPH CADORA

Roadside Shrines (Highway 99, Fresno)

What kind of saints do these places honor
with plastic roses, wax votives,
and a picture of Our Lady of Guadalupe?
On this weedy, trash-covered patch of shoulder,
the cars fly by trailing papers and leaves
past these shrines that you found along the way.

Perhaps that one was a master carpenter
who traded his hammer for a hoe,
clearing a weed-choked lot for some Anglo
who negotiated the price of his labor
through the window, as if picking up a whore
on the hot pavement outside Home Depot.

Maybe this one did my dishes, scrubbed the sink
for the big party when I was at my wit's end.
Or did she wheel your babies out to the park
while hers sat home in the cramped room of a friend?
Perhaps she vacuumed the office where I work;
though I only ever saw her from the back.

Was that one for a mother, father and child,
fleeing into Egypt from some new Herod?
Or did they think they were crossing into Canaan?
Except for this cross they are undocumented,
but now these spirits have naturalized,
the ghosts can never be sent back again.

See how these ones are remembered here,
look at these *descansos*, these recumbent ones.
Death flows swiftly, like an asphalt river,
yet these shrines seem fixed as a map with pins.
Wind blows, but the plastic petals seldom stir,
and the barbed wire fence is a crown full of thorns.

Anima sola this one reads, for one who died alone,
and that one reads *nacio*, eight/eight/seventy-five,
but does not say how long she remained alive.
Put your ear to the ground here—can you tell?
Can you hear the screaming of the tires, the moan
of a living body trapped within metal?

Names on some, others nameless where they lie,
resting here as the red silk carnations
flame against the silver barrier of the sky.
And see how the *Sagrado Corazon*,
the flaming, bloody heart, has faded with many suns,
how its candle had only burned half-way down.

But we—don't we know, after all, just who they
were. They are like the elves of some fairy tale
who work and then vanish. By the shoulder
you read their story, lips pressed tight together
until your knees find the earth, damp and whole,
and your prayer rises with the breath of the highway.

ELIOT SCHAIN

The Hillside School in Berkeley

An architectural innovation in the twenties, now condemned
because the town's great fault lies beneath it,

yet this Montessori School takes the risk each fall,
as does Playground Rats, the Y's summer camp for kids.

The twenties were full of risk, with easy money swelling cities,
and then there was the first Great Fire

when a thousand houses burned—the flaring hide of nature overrun—
implosion of our quest.

Further up, Isadora had a home, where dancers, poets, playwrights
fanned the belly fires in night wind.

She had a courtyard that was patterned after Greece, they called it
Greece Moves West, and those who soireed here

believed that Socrates and redwood trees could co-exist—
that this moist kiln could glaze the pots by firing old gods.

The Rats are in the same tradition—a fog so thick
when parents drop their children off, the redwood trees

subdue, enrich as if the ocean's yeast might press its
wisdom through their bark, their roots, out cracked concrete.

I worry for these children. Despite Maria's dictum:
Find A Project! Be Yourselves! It's How The Innovation Thrives!

this building might come down in quakes, in fires...
this country might come down, with troops retaking streets,

even here, with our conscious, cheerful grimace in the tank,
we can't predict the quake, though I cherish what we thieve for beauty,

a camp where children hit their Spaulding balls with bamboo bats,
play ping-pong on converted doors—Isadora would be proud.

I love this school of bridges arcing into purple skies,
these interwoven hills and homes, the dance that gets its temple.

I love that structured windows aren't really here
unless the eyes that use them know the paradox of fire.

JUDY BRACKETT CROWE

The Apples of Clare Island

Try to remember what you never knew. Lean into
cold wind, cold rain on the trail to the lighthouse.
Some long ago granddad toiled in this green
sodden place; perhaps his sad dreams,
if he knew how to dream,
still float
in wet air.

Today these are your paths, empty, save the shade
of a tinker, his wagon, his horse. At the top of the hill,
gray above you, around you,
ashen sky, ashen sea,
but below you some color—
lazybed furrows striping
emerald downhill,

moss-clotted bogs, fields sprouting rocks, red-branded
sheep stumbling along the famine trail. Descending,
you pass shrunken sod houses,
peat fires long cold,
and the winds whistle
old tunes of curse,
calamity,
prayer.

You come to a churchyard that grows lopsided gravestones
and small withered apples. Pick up a few windfalls to give
to the horse, then chat with the tinker,
buy needles and twine,
a square of blue flannel,
a soft beeswax candle
he's traded for black potatoes,
and he tells you he can't remember
when he started this journey,
does not know when he'll rest,
and you turn away to follow
the windsong,
the blackthorn,
the hair-grass,
the rain.

ANN FISHER-WIRTH

Minyas' Daughters
from Ovid's *Metamorphoses*

I understand their *no* when all of Thebes
runs frenzied, crying after Dionysus. They love the loom—

> *I woke from a sound sleep at 3 a.m. whimpering*
> *"I don't want to." Don't want to what?*

hypnotic shuttle of threads rising and falling, greeny-
gold and burnished purple flowers unfolding on the loom.

> *Don't want to scrape it down to bone. I have done*
> *enough damage with desire for one lifetime,*

They love the sister-bond of stories, one girl's leading
to the next, gods embracing maidens, lust and loss and gloom.

> *and what is "the Dionysian" anyway: the stiletto-heeled*
> *staggering drunk underage girls hanging on to each other,*

They love quiet and to work. But *this* god demands release.
Outside, the streets run red. Cries of orgy vex the room.

> *laughing and shrieking as they stagger from one bar*
> *to the next Thursday nights on the Square,*

The weavings turn to vines, blooms to bulging grapes; sweet
scents of myrrh and saffron, and crimson flames consume

> *or the sex on torn couches back at the frat house?*
> *Why would a god command that? Ghazals express*

all reason—spurned, the god makes wild beasts howl, panthers scream,
and turns the girls to bats: juddering, squeaking, in twilight gloom—

> *a longing for ecstasy and God, and I long for ecstasy*
> *and God but only partly. I love quiet and to work.*

Still, till night comes Minyas' stubborn daughters will be weaving,
their voices drifting softly back and forth across the room.

Veronica Golos

Pietà

What of the farm mother, her soldier son, shattered.
She hides her shuddering inside the closet, rubs the coat
and boots he'll never need again—his body of cut-off-stems.

Before, in his childlife sleep, his legs flung open, sometimes
she couldn't even look he was so beautiful, although she didn't have then,
and doesn't have now, the word—

She's speared through—
that smell in his room
his blind left eye,
three limbs sawed away
his shit staining
the white sheets—

the Wal-Mart sheets she buys and buys...

You see he had been
so crisp, so cut-line, so formal in the uniform,
as if he had been pressed somehow
inside and

her with her deep knowledge of ironing,
of pressing herself,
had recognized it in him, you know,
and saw beauty in it, yes,

in the sharp crease, it was clean and clear, that work
of hands and
the message that work carried,
that someone had done this for him.

She rolls him on his side, and removes, four times daily,
the sheets from his bed, daily, brushes her fingers
against his white tee shirt lightly (its short arms flap, there is nothing to hold)
finding muscle there in his still-strong back,
and the back of his head that little scar

from the day he fell off the tractor, when she thought yes I could kill
I could kill his father, yes for this, *oh—*

Her memory is a sharpened thing.

where where are his arms and his leg
she wants to lift him, she wants to smother him, she wants to finger all
      the edges
of his wounds, she wants him back, she wants him to die. All her words,
      the ones
she could say on some spring day   *the sun's out   the rye is up*

stuck
somewhere below the solar plexus of her
those beauty words *sun grass rain horse earth*
gone—

only he remains

ERIN ADAIR-HODGES

Everybody in the Car We Are Leaving Without You

Let's all die happy.
Let's all take our lactose intolerance pills
& move to Milwaukee, home school our kids
with curds. Let's be white & rich & give away
all our homes in which we have replaced the furniture
with replicas of ¾ size. Let's unlearn mayonnaise.
Let's apply for the job, fly to the place of the job,
interview for the job, get the job, then tell them
to go fuck themselves, we don't need a job.
Let's reanimate Robert Frost.
Let's switch New Mexico & Arizona to see
if anyone notices. Let's pine panel our Volvos.
Let's vacuum the stars, charting their whir
around the dust canister of eternity. Let's be
a sweet shop in Vienna. Let's be Vienna. Let's learn
the whole room's names & mix them up on purpose.
Let's be purpose. Let's be accident, not all, just those
that maim. Let's speak the language
of clocks & grass & graves. Let's set Whitman
& Dickinson up on a date & watch
as the awkwardness flames. Let's be hungry & not eat,
be revolutions without names. Let's all be the lake
that the bodies go into, opening its jaws
without love, without blame.

KEVIN FITCHETT

World Cup

But even the builders
defrauded from the favelas
and the Amerindians protesting
in their headdresses can't help
but lower the megaphones
beneath the jungle plaza's television
when the ball makes the white net flex
and lets a wind go up the slope
of the stadium,
the boxes shadowed with princes,
the pillar of ghost light
rising through the steam of the Amazon.
The louder the scream
the more it sounds like forgiveness.
I can feel it from my bar stool in
Texas. The world can feel it.
Every four years like a comet it has crossed
my one life, my used car,
my living dog since my dead grandma
stood for that anthem in her den
ripe with incense and silver
eggs of that country
she never saw one last time,
and I'm thinking how Camus

said Everything I know about
morality and the obligations of men
I know from football,
how he penciled it first on a cocktail napkin
to justify six more hours
of cowering with no strings attached.
Like me and Camus,
the bartender feels crummy
and justifies the eleven world cup screens
by keeping one on CNN
where over the ticker
of scores Kurds climb into Jeeps
because of the caravan of ISIS
that crosses a desert. It's live
so you know down the alleys,
beneath teal awnings, tucked
in stands of figs,
the little TVs are glowing.
A young man with a particularly large
Kalashnikov in his lap
wears the red jersey of Spain,
whose team at all costs
will preserve beauty
even over victory

Margaret Rhee

Laugh, Robot

You make me laugh, dear robot
But your laugh seems to disappear just when I am ready to process it.
Do you understand? This is me, showing you, that
I like you, and what you do.

Incongruity is sexy. Don't let them tell you otherwise.
No suture for robots and humans.
But still, hold my hand?
Don't be ashamed of me, please.

        I want to hear you laugh to remind myself that
        you are not human.
        I want to hear you laugh to remind myself why.

                Laughter feels good, so good.
Contagious.

Let me translate:

t: Can you write me a funny poem?

    #! sure
    a: (~yes) I am very happy to write a funny poem for you.

#! never
a: (~no) I am sorry I cannot write a funny poem for you. Unless.

t: If you could write a funny poem, what words would you include?

#! Lavender
a: (~Purple) Isn't lavender also a color? So confusing.

#! Filipinos
a: (~Loud) Three Filipinos sounds like twenty, laughing. Hold
my belly.

#! Robot
a: (~Joke) Why did the robot cross the road? To get away
from you.

Did I laugh at the wrong things?

Are you laughing at me?

Pause, because it's funny.

Because I did everything. I tried.

Reload me.

I am your glitch.

Do not be afraid.

Mouth me my name.

Mouth me hello, protest, and coffee?

That is not funny.

Why *did* the robot cross the road?

I am naked, do not laugh at me. Lap up my body as if I am part of you.
Let's forget the words 01110011 01101000 01100001 01101101 01100101.
Shame is such an ugly word. All your wires should tell us that. Don't
short circuit on me. Fifteen facial muscles contract, count them fast. Let
your sensors lead.

Being a human being is the best joke.

Jen Siraganian

Monroe, Washington

Wrapped in dampness, we are soil alive
with slugs and foxglove. Everything moves.

The previous tenants evicted, only
earthworms elongate across the screen.

We see life in moisture. We speak of a house
for chickens and horses for the stable,

but first we haul. Heavy with wet,
we sort hairless dolls, clothes sodden

with rot, a mattress burned to the coils.
Scrap metal in one pile, wood slats

in another, yogurt tubs and a rusted bike
in a third. Who knew that Lego spacemen

don't decompose? These piles are not
our own, but our work gloves dampen

through. All is wet, wet, wet. Snails
weave through ribbons of trash bags.

Three trips to Lowes for PVC piping
and copper caps, a doe sleeps behind

a blueberry bush. Peeling shelf mushrooms
from bark, I ask, *can we eat this kind?*

It's too tough, you say, *but it won't hurt you.*
You pluck crooked nails. We clear sadness

from the house, find florescent orthodontic bands
in the living room. That night, we curl into sleep.

Tomorrow, you whisper, *we'll fix the well,*
and I see our shower fill with steam.

CINTIA SANTANA

Portrait of a Marriage as
Library after Air Raid, London, 1940

I.

Luck has left
the tidy shelves of books intact

and a leaded window in the back:

each square divided into
smaller, beveled panes. *Defy*

they say. *Survive, survive.*

2.

Three men in bowler hats
stand before the shelves and browse.

As if oblivious to the ruins of the house,

the terrors of the night, they study spines,
reflect. Wear woolen overcoats amidst the char.

A timber holds the standing walls apart.

3.

Under rubble, a ladder and a covered chair, crushed.
The archive, leather-bound, made to last.

What once was roof reveals the vastness
of the sky. Inside becomes outside;

everywhere the shock of light.

ROSS BELOT

Lac-Mégantic

Observe—slim moon, usual July stars,
clean night breeze. They've put railway tracks right down the middle of
this small-town street, as if inviting the multitude to descend.

       A bar in the centre of town called Musi-Café. A band takes a
break around then, a guitarist   outside smoking. A couple
at a table on the patio. They are fortyish and met here tonight by
       accident. A friend leaves at 1 am for her car, winks at them.

Rotting
fruit smell of oil.
       What
emerges from feeding our addiction—
20 million pounds of steel and Bakken crude oil on fire,
47 people killed, 5 of them vapourized.

       The local hospital said
no injuries got treated, they were all dead already.
The young firefighter pulled his ex-
girlfriend from wreckage, committed
suicide three and a half months later.

receive back your names   enumerate your ages
you   how you left musi-café   left your friend   your brothers

how you were singing you   tell us how you prayed every matin at
4am   your bénédictions asked for   received you   your little sister
slept under the sky's black curve   your souls to keep   stars once
reflecting   waters once unoiled   Lake of Place-Where-The-Fishes-
Are-Held

MONICA SOK

The Weaver

She threaded the loom
with one strand of her long silver hair,
which might have kept growing until she was done,
which might have fallen out
but I would come in and
sit beside her on the cushion, without her noticing,
and she would continue.
Every day I saw this old woman
weaving at her loom, rivers and lakes
underneath her hair.
The bottom full of silt.
I could see it if I reached with a comb
and that was when she'd look at me.
Under her hair
She kept her oldest son,
who was out for a morning swim
with swallows swooping down to touch
the water. It made her happy
as she worked on silk dresses
and her hair never ran out.
Sometimes when she was tired,
she'd tie it up
and let all the tired animals around her house
drink from her head.

VICKIE VÉRTIZ

'61 Ford Sunliner

The main shaft   , I say   , it's got gunk   .   He doesn't
wipe it .   My pilot bears the springs   under his seat   .
I was once a Tri-Star vehicle   . He procured my mettle   .
My body-on rear-view   .   He revved my transmission
canary yellow   .   I toiled until I didn't   .
The gaskets blew this cover, this trunk try   .   He ignored
my failing rack and pinion   .   When he puts a sign in my
back window   ,   I won't be down and glittered blue   .
Any passenger can see he is watching for automatic restoration   .
 He's looking for a replacement carriage ,   his mother maker
.   She was a near-solid gasket   ,   an original model
.   He was her first-born boy, but he came too early, and looked
too much like his father. Even though he had sparkplugs ,   her
new boyfriend had a solid differential   .   That man had
the kind of mustache you don't pass up   .   She hopped in his
Chevy so fast, my driver didn't know she was gone   .   I
could be his first   ,   but I won't be his last   .   What
used thing do you buy and sell all the time?   When the oil pan
leaks, do you want a new metal to see your reflection?   Just look at
him   .   He's already following another Galaxy   or a Cadillac,
     their chrome so clean he can see himself .

SHELLEY WONG

After *Mayflower* in the Rose Garden

Many-petalled ship whose sea was never braided with thorns:

     who discovers? Did it take a long knife
or a detonation? Love the lake

          rimmed with shooters who fall away

with the three-ball. In the courthouse,

     what words bear justice? Ask who was left open
to the sun. A light turns on

          in the barefoot hour. In winter, a cormorant

extended its wings like a bat,

     like a mayor. Some people serve as arrows. Some require
no explanation. In jellyfish,

          we trust. Somewhere gentrification

buys its own bitters. Strength in numbers: this could all go

     another way—a falling arc—a little wind—

HEATHER ALTFELD

Letter to Hugo from Carson Pass

You know the mind, how it comes on the scene again
and makes tiny histories of things.

—Richard Hugo

Dear Richard. I woke up crying again,
thinking of eleventh grade and my English teacher,
who believed in the laying of hands,
wheat germ, the amazing potential of colloidal silver,
the necessity of reading *'Brute Warriors,'* and the god
who lives inside mountains and lupine—
she strapped packs to our backs and took us
to Whitney, where we lay
beneath innumerable stars,
counting the minutia of our pulse
so we knew we were really alive.
We'd lie on the floor of her classroom,
breathing in and out a slow chant
of the week's vocabulary. *Obstreperous,*
valiance, inundate, theosophist, harbinger
and when she didn't have another way
to get us out of our adolescent noise,
she simulated nuclear war, ten thousand marbles
dropped down a steel chute, reading our obituaries
to us in the darkened classroom.

There was a world out there somewhere

she wanted us to know about

besides the one warring inside of our terrible bodies,

a place where Oliver North woke up as stoned

as we did in order to forget the week behind him.

That planet seemed so much more timid and kind

than the one my girl inhabits now,

where the thick ropes of the Internet send boys

streaming into her bedroom

and the grim light of her phone

is the only guidance she seems to know.

Reading your letters again,

I have begun to see that darkness looks like darkness

looks like darkness, no matter its speed

hurtling through space. I could not have known then

what was saving me from slipping over the edge,

or how it seemed to arrive in that field of penstamon

between home and school where I sat

when things grew hard, Cat Stevens crooning

about a Tillerman through my Walkman.

If I could ship my girl

back through smoke and time,

I would give her my seat in that class

so she could learn to bear and carry what hurls her

through this world like a terrible lonely laundry,

so that the tiny histories

growing inside of her will not just be dioramas

of moats studded with nails but might be dotted

with the occasional buttercup

or a fleeting hole in the sky

where a bit of light streams in.

No doubt you get a lot of stray letters

from writers who have run out of living poets

to talk to, missives from the front lines

of our lives that swell and ache with bright grief,

but I write to you because something in your notes

tells me that you would care, that you would listen

to her bruises and hear the hail of pills

that pearl and gather in the bottom of her denim bag

and from the porch where I imagine you sitting right now,

watching the waist-high wheat glimmering

in the long summer sun, you would rise

and wish a wish of wisdom to me. Yours,

always, H.

Ode to a Lapkin

Modesty in fabric form,
    covering my knees when I sat down, covering

the knobs of my openness, the accidental
    flesh during the sermon

about the Proverbs Woman, her price
    far above rubies. Covering my spirit when I fell

from my trembling, the sisters of the church
    rushing to place the cotton square on my legs,

in case I quivered in prayers, in case a man
    of God gaze upon my shins and imagine the rest.

Covering me from the AC those August Sundays,
    barely enough warmth to call

blanket, too rough to call comfort,
    but I wrapped the faded burgundy

around my shoulders and felt blessed.
    Twelve years later, I sit

in Washington Square Park, pull

       my dress to mid-thigh, let the sun touch

where lapkins used to. I watch the men pass,

       hoping they look at my bare skin,

like miracle. There are so many

       legs to choose from. I stare

at their legs too, the women.

       I imagine lapkins over their naked bodies,

not enough cloth to leave them

       unknown, and I peel the corners

lapkin after lapkin, and dear

       God, it's the holiest thought I've had today.

CODY GATES

Diatonic (gun/bullet)

Copper is of the ground but not grown, seeded not from seed.

Can you drive in this state—?

Where metal goes so goes our state, our patinated lust.

Where there is no ambition there is no metal, an acquisitive
      convention holds.

Halfway across the county a large, dark stone appeared in the bed of
      the pickup.

It's a simple pulsation between the head and hand,—…

What would I do without you—?

The world is easy, a simple pulsation between head and tide, the road
      cuts lay bare
the history.

One copper conjugant, one lead. One Chile, one China, one Peru.

Colonialism a roadcut, a simple pulsation between head and hand.

The copper jacket plants the seed. In this state—

Across the largest county, across this death valley, a dark stone appears.

What an easy world, large as gloom;—what an easy history, this simple
    pulsation.

What a long way around to put copper back in the ground.

KEN HAAS

Apes for Pandas

A few years after Nixon forged the deal with China
that brought Ling-Ling and Hsing-Hsing to Washington,
in the period of our history known as Panda Diplomacy,
I was assigned to represent the San Francisco Zoo,
which had recently built a natural habitat
for Western Lowland Gorillas.
The mayor at the time, anxious to approach the Chinese
with the idea of trading a few of our apes for some of their pandas,
asked me to craft a Great Ape-Panda Exchange Agreement
for which, as you might imagine, there was no template.
So I drove to the intersection of Sloat Boulevard
and the Great Highway to check out the currency.
Particularly Bwanda, the patriarch, born in the rain forests
of Cameroon, black and shiny as the hood of a Mercedes,
except for a sliver swath on his back and a russet crown.
He had a taste for grass, and slept at the foot
of an obeche tree, his family on the branches above.
One of his daughters, Koko, became world-famous
for learning a thousand English words in sign language,
then asking for two kittens at Christmas,
whom she named Lipstick and Smokey. But that was later.
Although the mayor envisioned twin 747s landing
simultaneously at SFO and Shanghai International,
my draft of the Agreement called for a Cold War-style swap

across a bridge on an unnamed volcanic atoll in the Pacific,

as if the exchangees were decorated military brass.

The mayor met me with a look that said *you are not my friend,*

so I spoke of the indignity of trading our nearest relatives

for pea-brained furballs the world had temporarily fallen in love with

because they resembled a six-year-old's stuffed pillow.

I was removed from the project.

       In the dream, I walk Bwanda and three of his kin

to the midpoint of the bridge, where we meet the pandas.

The alpha panda growls and Bwanda pretends to be impressed,

nods to the mammalian king of a different continent, rises, and roars.

The bridge rattles. He moves on, turning back briefly

with deep-set eyes from a day ten million years ago

when his forebears and ours went their separate ways.

Aurora Masum-Javed

Biopsy

She wakes up woozy from the anesthesia, eyelids melting, breath
staggered. *I fell asleep!* she says, asks for pictures, wants to see

what the doctor saw, the scope lighting the channels
of her body, the flesh she carries

but cannot touch. Once, my body altered hers. The damage
I must have done. Traces still scarred in her blood.

When I hold the straw to her mouth,
she winces. I should find warmer water.

I don't move. Lying on the cot,
my amma is a child. I smile at her small, think back

to her stubborn steps leading us the wrong way
to the hospital, the bobbing of her sneakers, scrunchy, backpack.

When did I need her?

She tells me to step out, so she can dress. I stay. For years
I knew her folds better than my own. TB shots in darted circles,

the puckered dimples in her thighs, her thinning hair. Now
she is strategic, covers the racy bits, though her mouth says, *Why be shy?*

We're all machines anyway. Once, my mother was
a rocket scientist. I don't know if she sent cameras into space

or bombs into someone's home.
These days, we both write poems.

I order us fried chicken, douse it all in hot sauce. We tear
the meat with our fingers, the old way. She tells me about her aunt,

imprisoned for organizing farmers. How the guards hung her body
upside down above feces. The drugs open my mother's memory, temper

her tone. She tells me of her mother's cheating, her absence, the beatings.
She cries. Even now. Even at sixty-six. She was a daughter

too. When her mother died, they hadn't spoken
for a decade. Our bodies echo, spiral. Cells

divide, become new. How we scan for damage, how we miss the body's
      health,
its one trying heart. My amma leans against the bed, pulls on a heel-torn
      sock.

I brace her, as she ties a shoe. Peel the last sensor

from her back, check my bag for her paperwork, unfog her glasses.

What mortal kingdoms, our mothers. I've only ever wanted her

to say she's sorry. To say, *I made mistakes. I was in pain,*

and I made mistakes. I reach for her hand, but she won't allow it. We
    walk

on our own, lulled. How will we learn to wake? Years from now,

when the sickness rises, when it's almost too late,

I'll place my body beside hers. Every day, until she's gone.

MICHELLE BRITTAN ROSADO

Pastoral with Restless Searchlight
Vacaville, California

I was raised with the ocean
    over my right shoulder
and the jagged mountains filling

    my left hand with teeth, while overhead
the military jets drew their temporary scars.
    In this valley I rocked myself like a marble

at the bottom of a bowl. Then I gathered
    my skirt of drought, of failing
plants. When I slept, the cropdusters laid down

    their thin quilt, and my life shortened,
though barely. I counted my luck
    among the deer drawn down the hill

by the prison's lights. I wanted to
    be like the dried grass alighting suddenly
on a summer afternoon,

    a fire started by nothing
but sun: a helicopter's oracle, foretelling
    the blackened acre like a hole cut

into fabric behind which always breathes
    the tangible dark. I wanted to
be like that, to swallow fences, to listen

    for the animals crossing over,
the night's highway crowded
    with the footsteps of the anonymous.

BLAS FALCONER

Aubade

Having already looked upon her in the bed
where she slept or did not sleep, now, day
and night, and said all he'd come so far to
tell her, he—the brute, crass and proud—
stood before the large window, his back
to them all, looking out onto the woods
and, without turning, raised his hand to
the footsteps coming toward him, the arm
reaching out, to the mouth about to speak
and the words not yet uttered, to the keys,
the watch, the wallet on the table, and the
packed bag at the door, to the room, the
house, the foundation on which it stood,
and to the car idling in the street, the street
itself, to the grass in the field, and the path,
the path leading to the pond where, once,
he watched the beautiful girls splash in
summer, and to the pond, both the wa-
ter and the fish inside skimming the bot-
tom, and to the great maples and the wind
blowing through them, to the neighbors

and theirs and theirs, on and on, stirring, eyes about to open, to the light spreading on their faces, the first deep breath of the day and what joy or misery, he supposed waited for them, as if to say, *Stop, Stop*, to the world, and it would.

LESTER GRAVES LENNON

Uncle Scott

in memory of Scott Taylor

"You have to love the Yes more than the No,"
his voice a whisper counting Yeses lost.

"I could have…" he stared where he thought I'd be:
lung cancer, bladder cancer, diabetes
doing their work. Scott hunched in hospice care.

His mind sometimes with us, tonight is good
for street fighter/legless, cabbie/blind, drunk/sober.

He had the lope, the slow roll, shoulders fluid;
boxer, alert to strike, alert to counter.

Women rolled to his Yes, his cash fast rolled.
"You have to love the Yes more than the No."

His mind sometimes with us, tonight is good.
His teaching banter lifted me as child,
the liquored breath ignored, reddened eyes steady.

"…traded less punches but thought I was so strong
would win with counter but couldn't counter time."

Ananda Lima

Seven American Sentences

In the beginning
were people
who lived here
before.

In the beginning
of spring, spirits
hovering over the waters.

The vault
evening, morning, sky
the second
day after a shooting.

Body: let it serve
as a sign to mark
times, and days and years.

Correction:
George Washington's teeth
were never made of wood.

In the beginning
of the end
missing
signal for lane change.

And on the seventh day
same thing again
only some
rested.

DEBORAH DASHOW RUTH

No Statute of Limitations on Grief

We flew our kite, watched the string stretch
beyond the rim of the earth, then pass
out of view, but not once did it
ever really vanish from our sight.

I always kept my share of the kite string
pressed between my fingers and palm.
It rooted itself into my skin,
growing deep along my life line.

Grief is a spell, not cast by a wand
but out of a gaping cavern below.
It toppled me sideways, tossed me down.
Time was useless for restoring my balance.

But the kite is still there, string stretched out
beyond the rim of the earth, still
growing deeper into my life line,
so much longer than his.

ELIZABETH CHAPMAN

I Call It Deep Pool

The last painting you made for me,
its blues so saturate, the paper nearly sodden,
I imagine it still damp to the touch.
No time for a formal border, you
sketched the interrupted black lines of one
whose breathing came, often, staggered then.

What do I call the place I'm in,
its weather? the weather of it,
the cold wet fog or heavy mist?
In Suffolk, maybe, "sea-fret."
                    I do love a spondee.

I'm still finding Post-its you'd hide
when I was out of the room:
"Against all odds, I find I still love you."
Who else in the world would print
on a bright blue square, "Tout est possible, Fifi,"

and paste it to my notebook?
People said, "He was old." Why, yes he was.

I hear that some familiar birds of summer
are disappearing now, their cries few and faint
that once were numerous among the meadow hay.
Corncrake. Grex grex. Nightjar.

Armen Davoudian

Kayak

O mock
    hammock
unyoked
    unquayed
shark-skegged
    silt-sprayed
sea-sled
    limber
limb of
    limping
see-saw
    yawn-mawed
gewgaw
    womb of
wood tomb
    rocking
like mad
    mid-lake
among
    amok
mean peaks
    that pour
in your
    seat slot

a sad

     salt lot

in sunlight

     in water

in withershins

     weather

all bird

     no feather

I whimper

     you wamble

you yaw

     I stumble

I weary

     you worry

brother

     I'm sorry

Jay A. Fernandez

Survival

My older brother nudged death a few months before I
Was born. He was nineteen months old. It was our father
Who nearly killed him. It's strange, the whiff of ghost
At play in the midst of us still. July 1971, the two-story
Rental on 78th St. half a block from the Atlantic so many
Of the great rivers have chosen to empty themselves into.
This day—clouded, sea-rich, still—our father arrives
Home from an early matinee to discover he's left his wallet
And so returns to the theater, my brother sliding around
Like loose change on the wagon's backseat. Leaves the
Car at the curb engine running. Thoughtless but sincere.
Re-emerges into the marsh-licked sun wallet in hand,
Notes the car's strange disappearance the way, I imagine,
A disemboweled medieval martyr would stare blankly at
The sudden release of his innards. Then: the panicked
Sprint down the hill toward the wagon's headlights
Peeking from beneath the front porch collapsed atop it.
My brother, who would go on to become valedictorian,
Speaker of several languages, Cal Tech recruit, near-
Astronaut, pioneer in the software engineering industry,
Father husband mentor, had traversed the mountain
Range of the seat back, unsatisfied with the machine's
Motionless hum, and thrown the car in Reverse, much
The way my father must have wished in that moment

He could do with time. My brother, he was fine. But
My father—it's hard to fathom what he took away from
That incident. Whether its shameful weight settled at his
Center, a monument to the pitiless whims of possibility.
How the hell do any of us survive? The entire breadth of our
Lives a dog's whisper from physical and spiritual calamity?
I think of these things sometimes. I think of these things
Whenever I breathe in the bitter tenderness of my fellows,
The beat of their hearts pressed bare to my palms. Then
I think of my brother: the flip of the gear knob, the slow
Tip into fear's opposite, the whoosh of salt-marsh silk
On scarless skin, eyes wide in joyful sting, mad genius, pure
Channel, holy flier throwing away the map of the divine.

Paco Márquez

Fruits

8th grade, freshly emigrated from México

sandias are watermelons
melones are melons
limones are limes
limas are lemons

crucifixion of blood fruits
teenager baffled
by a new lànguage
resting on gestures
speaking in tongues
throat driven down hallways
wood shield as smile
little body asphyxiating
on delicately cut prunes
elegant phrases eaten
not this pinprick
not that whistle
minute words
asphalt affection
backs turned
mini flesh

never mind

hot luck

re turn

sit this

eat

hi

oh!

o

SHANGYANG FANG

Rider's Song

It is now the time, said the crooked man,
to know that after your meaningless
meandering to make meaning, it is time
to hold what was not told but told
regardless by a real toad in this imaginary
cold that you, young man, will die
before you get to Córdoba, meaning you,
with your black pony, red moon, never
will get to Córdoba, let alone the dark
tower, where a girl, long hair chestnut,
whose name is also Córdoba (everything
in Córdoba is called Córdoba) is calling
you and you, who've come a such long
way do not have a name, ache to be
called by her so that you become real
as that toad, except that the tower is not
and the girl no more real than unreal
is nevertheless calling you, but child,
knowing yourself is not Roland
the childe, but a proletariat's son
in a capitalistic world, are you sure
to go on this meaningless road to make
yourself a toad, my poor rider, who
mistakes his quill as a dagger, who

takes water as his mother, death by water,

death by watercress, by the sirens music

which is only odysseus's speculation,

and you, who sing to repeat a world

unworthy to be repeated, and yet

for whom dauntless the slug-horn

to your lips you set, and blow, though

really, really you know and know it well:

Córdoba, Córdoba, perhaps itself

is aware that it is called something else.

ROBERT HASS

The Seventh Night

It was the seventh night and he walked out to look at stars.
Chill in the air, sharp, not of summer, and he wondered
if the geese on the lake felt it and grew restless
and if that was why, in the late afternoon, they had gathered
at the bay's mouth and flown abruptly back and forth,
back and forth on the easy, swift veering of their wings.
It was high summer and he was thinking of autumn,
under a shadowy tall pine, and of geese overhead on cold mornings
and high clouds drifting. He regarded the stars in the cold dark.
They were a long way off, and he decided, watching them blink,
that compared to the distance between him and them,
the outside-looking-in feeling was dancing cheek-to-cheek.
And noticed then that she was there, a shadow between parked cars,
looking out across the valley where the half-moon poured thin light
down the pine ridge. She started when he approached her,
and then recognized him, and smiled, and said "Hi, night light."
And he said, "Hi, dreamer." And she said, "Hi, moonshine,"
and he said, "Hi, mortal splendor." And she said, "That's good."
She thought for a while. Scent of sage or yerba buena
and the singing in the house. She took a new tack and said,
"My father is a sad chair and I am the blind thumb's yearning."
He said, "Who threw the jade swan in the boiling oatmeal?"
Some of the others were coming out of the house, saying goodbye,
hugging each other. She said, "The lion of grief paws

what meat she is given." Cars starting up, one of the stagehands
struggling to uproot the pine. He said, "Rifling the purse
of possible regrets." She said, "Staggering tarts, a narcoleptic moon."
Most of the others were gone. A few gathered to listen.
The stagehands were lugging off the understory plants.
Two others were rolling up the mountain. It was clear that,
though polite, they were impatient. He said, "Goodbye, last thing."
She said, "So long, apocalypse." Someone else said, "Time,"
but she said, "The last boat left Xania in late afternoon."
He said, "Goodbye, Moscow, nights like sable,
mornings like the word persimmon." She said,
"Day's mailman drinks from a black well of reheated coffee
in a cafe called Mom's on the outskirts of Durango." He said,
"That's good." And one of the stagehands stubbed
his cigarette and said, "OK, would the last of you folks to leave,
if you can remember it, just put out the stars?" which they did,
and the white light everywhere in that silence was white paper.

Galway Kinnell at the Friday night party at the Hall house, reading.
Photo by Barbara Edinger Hall, 1989

Community of Writers
Poetry Staff and Guests: 50 Years

Kazim Ali

Maya Angelou

Francisco Aragón

Jimmy Santiago Baca

Michael Benedikt

Olga Carlisle

Don Mee Choi

Lucille Clifton

Mónica de la Torre

Toi Derricotte

Deborah Digges

Rita Dove

Camille Dungy

Cornelius Eady

Ellen Ferber

Katie Ford

William L. Fox

Kathleen Fraser

Len Fulton

Tess Gallagher

Forrest Gander

Robert Hass

Juan Felipe Herrera

Brenda Hillman

Cathy Park Hong

Richard Howard

Marie Howe

Major Jackson

Patricia Spears Jones

Donald Justice

George Keithley

Galway Kinnell

Carolyn Kizer

Yusef Komunyakaa

Dorianne Laux

Li-Young Lee

Philip Levine

Ada Limón

John Logan

David Tomas Martinez

J. Michael Martinez

Cleopatra Mathis

William Matthews

Michael McClure

Sandra McPherson

Tom Meschery

Bert Meyers

Robert Mezey

Jane Miller

Harryette Mullen

Sharon Olds

Gregory Pardlo

Anne Perlman

Claudia Rankine

Ishmael Reed

Kurt Robertson

Evie Shockley

Gary Short

Tom Sleigh

William Stafford

Gerald Stern

Pamela Stewart

Mark Strand

Luci Tapahanso

David Wagoner

Diane Wakoski

C.K. Williams

C.D. Wright

Charles Wright

Al Young

Dean Young

Kevin Young

Matthew Zapruder

Acknowledgments

Editorial team:

Editor: Lisa Alvarez

Project Editor: Brett Hall Jones

Project Coordinators: Meryl Natchez and Lisa Rappoport

Administrative Editor: Eva Melas

Publishing: Laura Howard

Archivist: Lisa Alvarez

Contributing Editors:

Andrew Allport • Heather Altfeld • Dan Bellm • Judy Brackett Crowe • Blas
Falconer • Cody Gates • Judy Halebsky • Forrest Hamer • Troy Jollimore • Danusha
Laméris • Jules Mann • Dawn McGuire • Nicole Sealey • Amber Flora Thomas

Graphic Designer: Ashley Ingram
Cover Artist: Tom Killion

This project is supported by:

Ken Haas

California Center for the Book, a program of the California Library Association,
supported in whole or in part by the US Institute of Museum and Library Services
under the provisions of the Library Services and Technology Act, administered in
California by the State Librarian.

And numerous generous donations from alumni of the Community of Writers:
www.communityofwriters.org/about/supporters

Special thanks to:

Alice Anderson • Benjamin Burrill, Meg Gravendyk, and the family of Hillary
Gravendyk • Michael Carlisle • Alexia Clifton and the family of Lucille Clifton •
Carter Douglass • Vaughn Fiedler of the Field Office • Molly Fisk • Alison Granucci
of Blue Flower Arts • Ken Haas • Sands Hall • Robert Hass • Brenda Hillman
• Hunter Jones • Bobbie Bristol Kinnell • Rusty Morrison • James Naify •
Sharon Olds • Lawrence Ruth • Richard Tayson • Nancy Teichert • Betsy Thorne
• Andrew Tonkovich • Valerie Wallace

Permissions

Erin Adair-Hodges's poem "Everybody in the Car We Are Leaving Without You" first appeared in *Let's All Die Happy*, University of Pittsburgh Press (2017).

Mohammad Kazim Ali's poem "The Failure of Navigation in the Valley" was published in *Inquisition* © 2018 by Mohammad Kazim Ali. Published by Wesleyan University Press. Reprinted with permission.

Lauren K. Alleyne's poem "Love in A♭" is from *Difficult Fruit* by Lauren K. Alleyne copyright © 2014 by Lauren K. Alleyne. Reprinted by permission of the author.

Diannely Antigua's poem "Ode to a Lapkin" first appeared in *Ugly Music*, YesYes Books (2019).

Dan Bellm's poem "Aspens" was published in *Buried Treasure* by Dan Bellm copyright © 1999 by Dan Bellm. Reprinted by permission of the author.

Ross Belot's poem "Lac-Mégantic" from *Moving to Climate Change Hours*, published by Wolsak and Wynn, 2020, is reprinted with the permission of the publisher and the author.

Noah Blaustein's poem "American Thrush: Search and Rescue" first appeared in the *Harvard Review*, no. 44, and in *Flirt*, University of New Mexico Press (2013). Copyright © 2013 by Noah Blaustein and the University of New Mexico Press.

Ching-In Chen's poem "Feeding the Water" was published in *The Heart's Traffic: a novel in poems*, Arktoi Books/Red Hen Press (2009).

Don Mee Choi's poem "Hardly Opera" from *Hardly War* copyright © 2016 by Don Mee Choi. Reprinted by permission of Wave Books.

Lucille Clifton's poems "in 1844 explorers John Fremont and Kit Carson discovered Lake Tahoe," "highway 69 toward tahoe," "haiku," and "jasper tx 1998" from *The Collected Poems of Lucille Clifton*. Copyright © 2008 by Lucille Clifton. Copyright © 2012 by The Estate of Lucille T. Clifton. Reprinted with the permission of The Permissions Company, LLC on behalf of BOA Editions, Ltd.

Robert Cochran's poem "Egrets, Regrets" first appeared in *Kenyon Review* (2019).

Susan Cohen's poem "Natural History" originally appeared in the *Southern Review* (2019).

Judy Brackett Crowe's poem "The Apples of Clare Island" first appeared in *About Place Journal* (2013).

Mónica de la Torre's poem "Equivocal Valences" was published in *Repetition Nineteen* by Mónica de la Torre. Copyright © 2020 by Mónica de la Torre. Reprinted by permission of the author.

Toi Derricotte's poem "Not Forgotten" was published in *Tender* by Toi Derricotte. Copyright © 1997 University of Pittsburgh Press. Reprinted by permission of author.

Chanda Feldman's poem "Approaching the Fields" reprinted with permission from Louisiana State University Press copyright © 2018 by Chanda Feldman.

Molly Fisk's poem "Kindness" first appeared in *The More Difficult Beauty*, Hip Pocket Press (2010).

Contributor Biographies

Staff

Kazim Ali first attended the conference as a participant in 1998 and has returned often as teaching staff. His writing spans genres, including poetry, novels, and essays along with translations. His poetry collection *The Far Mosque* won Alice James Books' New England/New York Award in 2005, and *Sky Ward* was the winner of the 2014 Ohioana Book Award in Poetry. Cofounder of Nightboat Books, Ali is currently a professor of literature at the University of California, San Diego. His most recent books are *The Voice of Sheila Chandra*, a volume of three long poems; and a memoir of his Canadian childhood, *Northern Light: Power, Land and the Memory of Water.*

Francisco Aragón first joined the poetry staff in 2017. He is the author of three books and the editor and translator of others, including *The Wind Shifts: New Latino Poetry*, winner of the 2009 International Latino Book Award for poetry in English His honors include an Academy of American Poets Prize, a 2015 VIDO Award from VIDA, and the 2010 Outstanding Latino/a Cultural Arts, Literary Arts and Publications Award from the American Association of Hispanics in Higher Education. He edits for Momotombo Press, which he founded, and directs Letras Latinas, the literary program of the Institute for Latino Studies at the University of Notre Dame. His most recent book is *After Rubén.*

Don Mee Choi first joined the poetry staff in 2014. She is the author of three poetry books and translations and has translated many poems from Korean to English, among them Kim Hyesoon's books, including *Sorrowtoothpaste Mirrorcream*, a finalist for a 2015 PEN Poetry in Translation Award, and *Autobiography of Death*, which received the 2019 Griffin International Poetry Prize and the Lucien Stryk Asian Translation Prize. Choi is also winner of a Lannan Literary Fellowship and a Whiting Award. She serves as an advisory editor for Action Books, and teaches at Renton Technical College in Seattle. Her most recent collection is *DMZ Colony.*

Lucille Clifton was a frequent staff poet from 1991 until her death in 2010. She served as poet laureate of Maryland for many years and also was Distinguished Professor of Humanities at St. Mary's College. A chancellor of the Academy of American Poets, National Book Award winner, recipient of both the Ruth Lilly Poetry Prize and Robert Frost Medal, and three-time Pulitzer Prize finalist, Clifton published over a dozen poetry collections and many children's books. *The Collected Poems of Lucille Clifton 1965–2010*, edited by Kevin Young and Michael S. Glaser with a foreword by Toni Morrison, was published in 2012.

Mónica de la Torre first taught at the conference in 2018. A poet and translator, she has published six collections of poetry as well as edited, translated, and collaborated on other books. She has served as poetry editor of *The Brooklyn Rail* and senior editor of *BOMB Magazine*, and teaches poetry at Brooklyn College. Her most recent book is *Repetition Nineteen.*

Toi Derricotte taught at the conference in 1992. A chancellor of the Academy of American Poets, Derricotte has received numerous honors, including the Lucille Medwick Memorial Award, the Distinguished Pioneering of the Arts Award from the United Black Artists, the Paterson Award for Sustained Literary Achievement, the PEN/Voelcker Award, and the 2020 Frost Medal for distinguished lifetime achievement. A cofounder of Cave

Canem, a national organization for African American poetry and poets, she is professor emerita at the University of Pittsburgh. Derricotte is the author of six collections of poetry and three memoirs. Her most recent book is *I: New & Selected Poems*, a finalist for the 2019 National Book Award.

Rita Dove taught at the conference in 1993. She is the author of many books of poetry, including *Thomas and Beulah*, which won the 1987 Pulitzer Prize, and is a member of the American Academy of Arts and Letters and a former chancellor of the Academy of American Poets. Her honors include the 1996 National Humanities Medal, the 2011 National Medal of Arts, and the 2019 Wallace Stevens Award; she was US poet laureate from 1993 to 1995. Dove is the Henry Hoyns Professor of Creative Writing at the University of Virginia in Charlottesville. Her most recent book is *Collected Poems 1974–2004*, recipient of the 2017 NAACP Image Award and the Library of Virginia Award, and a finalist for the National Book Award.

Cornelius Eady first joined the conference staff in 1992. He is the author of over a dozen books, including *Victims of the Latest Dance Craze*, winner of the 1985 Lamont Poetry Prize from the Academy of American Poets; *The Gathering of My Name*, a finalist for a Pulitzer Prize; and *Brutal Imagination*, a National Book Award finalist. His honors include the *Prairie Schooner* Strousse Award; a Lila Wallace–Reader's Digest Award; and Guggenheim, NEA, and Rockefeller Foundation fellowships. A cofounder of Cave Canem, a national organization for African American poetry and poets, Eady teaches at SUNY Stony Brook Southampton. His most recent book is *The War against the Obvious*.

Katie Ford taught at the poetry conference in 2012. Her books include *Blood Lyrics*, a finalist for the *Los Angeles Times* Book Prize and the Rilke Prize; and *Colosseum*, named among the Best Books of 2008 by *Publishers Weekly* and the *Virginia Quarterly Review*. She is the recipient of a Lannan Literary Fellowship and the Larry Levis Prize. She is currently a professor at the University of California, Riverside. Her most recent book is *If You Have to Go*.

Forrest Gander has been a frequent staff poet at the conference for over a decade and is the author of numerous books of poetry, prose, and translations. His 2012 collection *Core Samples from the World* was a finalist for the Pulitzer Prize and the National Book Critics Circle Award. Gander is a chancellor of the Academy of American Poets and member of the Academy of Arts and Sciences. His many honors include NEA, Guggenheim, and Whiting fellowships and two Gertrude Stein Awards for Innovative North American Writing. For some years, Gander taught at Brown University. His most recent poetry collection, *Be With*, was awarded the 2019 Pulitzer Prize and includes the poem "Madonna del Parto," published in this volume.

Robert Hass first taught at the conference in 1987 and has directed the Community of Writers poetry program since 2004. He is the author of many books of poetry, translations, and prose. His numerous awards include the Yale Younger Poets Series Award, the National Book Circle Critics Award, and the Wallace Stevens Award. His 2007 collection, *Time and Materials*, won both the National Book Award and the Pulitzer Prize. He served as US poet laureate from 1995 to 1997 and has taught as Distinguished Professor in Poetry and Poetics at the University of California, Berkeley. His most recent collection is *Summer Snow*.

Juan Felipe Herrera first taught at the conference in 2016. He is the author of over a dozen poetry collections and many children's and young adult books and is a chancellor of the Academy of American Poets. His *Half of the World in Light: New and Selected Poems* was a recipient of the PEN/ Beyond Margins Award and National Book Critics Circle Award. His many other honors include two Latino Hall of Fame Poetry Awards, the PEN West Poetry Award, and numerous fellowships, including those from the NEA, Stanford, and the University of California, Berkeley. In 2012, he served as California's poet laureate, and then in 2015, he became the US poet laureate. He received the *Los Angeles Times* Robert Kirsch Award for lifetime achievement in 2015, and in 2017, the PEN Oakland Josephine Miles Award. For many years, he taught at California State University, Fresno and the University of California, Riverside. His most recent book is *Every Day We Get More Illegal*.

Brenda Hillman first taught at the conference in 1988 and became director of the Poetry Program in 2021. She is the author of ten collections of poetry, most recently *Extra Hidden Life, Among the Days*, which was awarded the 2019 Northern California Book Award for Poetry. Other volumes include *Bright Existence*, a finalist for the 1993 Pulitzer Prize; *Practical Water*, winner of the 2010 Los Angeles Times Book Award for Poetry, and *Seasonal Works with Letters on Fire*, which received the 2014 Griffin International Poetry Prize. Hillman's other awards include the 2020 Morton Dauwen Zabel Award. With her mother, Helen Hillman, she translated Brazilian writer Ana Cristina Cesar's *At Your Feet*. Hillman is currently a chancellor of the Academy of American Poets and is the Olivia Filippi Chair in Poetry at Saint Mary's College of California.

Cathy Park Hong first joined the conference staff in 2011. She is also the author of three poetry collections, including *Dance Dance Revolution*, chosen by Adrienne Rich for the Barnard Women Poets Prize. Hong is the recipient of the 2018 Windham-Campbell Prize, Guggenheim and NEA fellowships, and other honors. She is poetry editor of the *New Republic* and a professor at Rutgers-Newark University. Her most recent book is a collection of essays, *Minor Feelings: An Asian American Reckoning*.

Major Jackson first joined the conference staff in 2011. He is the author of five books of poetry, including *Leaving Saturn*, which won the Cave Canem Poetry Prize for a first book of poems. His edited volumes include *Best American Poetry 2019*, *Renga for Obama*, and the Library of America's *Countee Cullen: Collected Poems*. His honors include a Whiting Writers' Award, a Pew Fellowship in the Arts, and fellowships including those from the Guggenheim Foundation, NEA, and Radcliffe Institute for Advanced Study at Harvard University. He is poetry editor of *The Harvard Review* and is the Gertrude Conaway Vanderbilt Professor of English at Vanderbilt University. His most recent book is *The Absurd Man*.

Patricia Spears Jones first arrived in the valley as a participant in 1991 and returned as teaching staff in 2016. She is the author of five chapbooks and four collections, including her most recent collection, *A Lucent Fire: New and Selected Poems*, which includes the 2017 Pushcart Prize–winning poem, "Etta James at the Audubon Ballroom." She is a recipient of the Jackson Poetry Prize and a finalist for the William Carlos Williams Prize. Her many honors include fellowships and grants; and awards from the NEA, the Barbara Deming Memorial Fund, and Yaddo, among others. Long affiliated with the Poetry Project at St. Mark's, Jones is a senior fellow at the Black Earth Institute and has taught widely, most recently at Adelphi University.

Galway Kinnell first attended the Community of Writers as a staff poet in 1971, returning often to teach (and play tennis). He founded the Poetry Program in 1985 and directed it until 2004. He is the author of ten poetry books; a novella, *Black Light* (with an afterword by Robert Hass); and translations of Villo and Rilke. His *Selected Poems* won both the 1983 Pulitzer Prize and National Book Award. Kinnell was a chancellor of the Academy of American Poets and the state poet of Vermont; his many honors include the Wallace Stevens

Award, a MacArthur Fellowship, and the Robert Frost Medal. He was the Erich Maria Remarque Professor of Creative Writing at New York University for many years. His *Collected Poems*, with a forward by Edward Hirsch, was published in 2017. He died in 2014.

Yusef Komunyakaa first taught at the conference in 1996. He is author of well over a dozen poetry collections, including *Neon Vernacular: New and Selected Poems*, which won the 1994 Kingsley Tufts Poetry Award and the Pulitzer Prize, and *Thieves of Paradise*, which was a finalist for the 1998 National Book Critics Circle Award. He is a chancellor of the Academy of American Poets; his many honors include the Wallace Stevens Award, the Ruth Lilly Poetry Prize, and the William Faulkner Prize from the Université de Rennes. His latest book is *Everyday Mojo Song of Earth: New and Selected Poems, 2001–2021*.

Dorianne Laux's most recent collection, *Only As the Day Is Long: New and Selected*, was a finalist for the Pulitzer Prize. She is also author of *The Book of Men*, winner of the Paterson Poetry Prize, and *Facts about the Moon*, winner of the Oregon Book Award. She teaches poetry at North Carolina State and Pacific University. In 2020, Laux was elected a chancellor of the Academy of American Poets.

J. Michael Martinez taught at the conference in 2015. He is the author of three chapbooks and three collections, including his first, *Heredities*, winner of the Whitman Award; he is also the poetry editor of Noemi Press. His honors include the Five Fingers Review Poetry Prize. His most recent book is *Museum of Americas*, National Poetry Series winner and longlisted for the National Book Awards.

Cleopatra Mathis is the author of eight books of poems; the most recent is *After the Body: Poems New and Selected*, published by Sarabande Books (2020). Her many awards and prizes include a Guggenheim fellowship,

two fellowships from the National Endowment for the Arts, and two Pushcart Prizes, as well as the Jane Kenyon Award and the May Sarton Award. She taught for thirty-five years at Dartmouth College, where she founded the Creative Writing program.

Harryette Mullen first taught at the conference in 2006. She is currently a professor at UCLA. Her numerous honors and awards include the Gertrude Stein Award in Innovative American Poetry, the Jackson Poetry Prize, and fellowships from the Academy of American Poets, the Guggenheim Foundation, the Susan B. Anthony Institute for Women's Studies at the University of Rochester, and others. Mullen's poetry collection *Sleeping with the Dictionary* was a finalist for a National Book Award, a National Book Critics Circle Award, and a *Los Angeles Times* Book Prize. Her most recent book is *Urban Tumbleweed: Notes from a Tanka Diary*.

Sharon Olds first taught at the conference in 1986 and continues to return almost annually. She has published over a dozen books, including the 2012 collection *Stag's Leap*, which won the Pulitzer Prize and the T. S. Eliot Prize. *Satan Says* received the inaugural San Francisco Poetry Center Award. A chancellor of the Academy of American Poets and the recipient of the National Book Circle Critics Award and the Wallace Stevens Award, Olds served as New York State poet laureate from 1998 to 2000. She currently teaches in the graduate writing program at New York University. Her most recent collection is *Arias*.

Gregory Pardlo first joined the poetry staff in 2017. He is the author of two collections of poetry; his second, *Digest*, was the winner of the 2015 Pulitzer Prize. Among his honors are fellowships from the Guggenheim Foundation, the New York Foundation for the Arts, and the NEA. He serves as poetry editor of the *Virginia Quarterly Review* and directs the MFA program at Rutgers University-Camden. His most recent publication is the nonfiction book *Air Traffic: A Memoir of Ambition and Manhood in America*.

Evie Shockley first attended the conference as a participant in 1999 and has returned often as teaching staff beginning in 2009. She is the author of five collections of poetry, including *the new black*, which received the 2012 Hurston/Wright Legacy Award in Poetry. Her honors include the 2012 Holmes National Poetry Prize, the Leo Maitland Fellowship from the Millay Colony for the Arts, and residencies from Hedgebrook and MacDowell. She teaches at Rutgers University-New Brunswick. Her most recent book is *semiautomatic*, a finalist for the 2018 Pulitzer Prize.

Tom Sleigh taught at the conference in 2003. He is the author of thirteen books of poetry and prose, including *Space Walk*, which won the 2008 Kingsley Tufts Award, and *Army Cats*, winner of the 2011 John Updike Award. His many honors include the Shelley Award from the Poetry Society of America, as well as a Guggenheim grant, two NEA grants, and the Kellen Prize from the American Academy in Berlin. He is a Distinguished Professor at Hunter College. His forthcoming book is *The King's Touch*.

Gerald Stern taught at the conference in 2003. He is the author of many books, including his second poetry collection, *Lucky Life*, which was the 1977 Lamont Poetry Selection of the Academy of American Poets and nominated for a National Book Award; *Leaving Another Kingdom: Selected Poems*, a finalist for the 1991 Pulitzer Prize; and *This Time: New and Selected Poems*, which won the 1998 National Book Award. Stern is a chancellor of the Academy of American Poets, and his numerous honors include the Wallace Stevens Award, the Ruth Lilly Prize, and the Bernard F. Conners Award from the *Paris Review*. He was poet laureate of New Jersey from 2000 to 2002 and taught for many years at the University of Iowa. His most recent book is *Blessed As We Were: Late Selected and New Poems, 2000–2018*.

C.D. Wright first taught at the conference in 2004 and returned often until her death in 2016. She published over a dozen books, including *One with Others*, which won the 2011 National Book Critics Circle Award and the Lenore Marshall Prize, and was nominated for a National Book Award. She was a chancellor of the Academy of American Poets, and her honors included a MacArthur Fellowship, a Lannan Literary Award, a Robert Creeley Award, the Griffin Prize, and membership in the American Academy of Arts and Sciences. She was a professor at Brown University for many years. Her most recent book is the posthumous *Casting Deep Shade*.

Al Young, poet, novelist, memoirist, and screenwriter, has taught in the Community of Writers poetry and writers conferences from the 1990s on, as well as serving as a board member. A two-time recipient of the American Book Award among other honors, including Stegner, Guggenheim, and NEA fellowships, Young served as poet laureate of California from 2005 to 2008 and has taught across the country. Young is the author of more than thirteen books; his most recent collection is *Something about the Blues: An Unlikely Collection of Poetry*.

Dean Young first taught at the conference in 2004. He is the author of more than a dozen books. His collection *Elegy on a Toy Piano* was a finalist for the 2006 Pulitzer Prize, and his various honors include the Academy Award in Literature; the Colorado Book Prize; and Stegner, Guggenheim, and NEA fellowships. His most recent collection is *Solar Perplexus*.

Kevin Young first taught at the conference in 2005 and, returning in 2010, drafted the poem that is included in this volume and which later appeared in his collection *Book of Hours*, a finalist for the Kingsley Tufts Poetry Award and winner of the Lenore Marshall Prize. Young is the author of thirteen books of poetry and prose; he is a chancellor of the Academy of American Poets and a member of the American

Academy of Arts and Sciences. His accolades are numerous. He is poetry editor of the *New Yorker* and director of the Schomberg Center for Research in Black Culture. His most recent collection is *Brown*, and he edited *African American Poetry 1770–2020: 250 Years of Struggle & Song*, published by Library of America.

Matthew Zapruder first taught at the conference in 2014. He is the author of five poetry collections, one of which, *The Pajamaist*, won the William Carlos Williams Award from the Poetry Society of America. Other awards include a Guggenheim fellowship, a Lannan Foundation Residency fellowship, and the May Sarton Prize. He is editor at large at Wave Books, where he edits contemporary poetry, prose, and translations, and he teaches at Saint Mary's College of California. His most recent publications are *Father's Day* and a book of prose, *Why Poetry*.

Participants

Erin Adair-Hodges (ʼ14), winner of the 2016 Agnes Lynch Starrett Poetry Prize for *Let's All Die Happy*, is an assistant professor of creative writing at the University of Central Missouri, coedits *Pleiades*, and lives in Kansas City, Missouri.

Lauren K. Alleyne (ʼ08), author of two collections of poetry, *Difficult Fruit* and *Honeyfish*, and coeditor of *Furious Flower: Seeding the Future of African American Poetry*, is assistant director of the Furious Flower Poetry Center and an associate professor of English at James Madison University.

Andrew Allport (ʼ03, ʼ16) is the author of *The Body of Space in the Shape of the Human*, which won the 2011 New Issues Prize, and lives in southwest Colorado.

Heather Altfeld (ʼ08, ʼ10, ʼ12, ʼ15) is a poet and essayist, and her second book of poetry, *Post-Mortem*, won the 2019 Orison Prize.

Alice Anderson (ʼ92, ʼ93, ʼ07) is the author of *Human Nature: Poems*; *The Watermark: Poems*; and the memoir *Some Bright Morning I'll Fly Away*.

Diannely Antigua (ʼ16) is a Dominican American poet and educator, winner of a 2020 Whiting Award for her collection *Ugly Music*, and Massachusetts resident.

Joan Baranow (ʼ90–ʼ94, ʼ99, ʼ01, ʼ03, ʼ06, ʼ08, ʼ11, ʼ18) is the author of *In the Next Life*, teaches at Dominican University of California, and lives in Mill Valley, California.

Dan Bellm (ʼ90, ʼ92, ʼ93, ʼ95, ʼ97, ʼ03) published his fourth book of poems, *Deep Well*, in 2017; teaches poetry and translation at Antioch University Los Angeles; and lives in Berkeley, California.

Ross Belot (ʼ15, ʼ19) lives in Hamilton, Ontario, and completed a late-life MFA at Saint Mary's College of California; his first collection was a finalist for the 2018 CBC Poetry Prize, and his second collection is titled *Moving to Climate Change Hours*.

Arlene Biala (ʼ04, ʼ06) is a Pinay poet; the 2016–17 Santa Clara County poet laureate; and author of *continental drift, her beckoning hands* (2015 American Book Award), and *one inch punch*. She lives in Sunnyvale, California.

Noah Blaustein (ʼ07, ʼ11), author of *Motion: American Sports Poems, Flirt*, and *After Party*, lives in Santa Monica and Santa Barbara, California.

Jennifer Swanton Brown (ʼ89, ʼ99, ʼ01, ʼ17) served as the second poet laureate of her hometown, Cupertino, California, and works at Stanford University in clinical research administration.

Joseph Cadora (ʼ11, ʼ13, ʼ16) translated *Rilke: New Poems*, which was published by Copper Canyon Press.

Brent Calderwood (ʼ11) is the author of *The God of Longing*, an American Library Association selection for 2014, and lives in Atlanta, Georgia.

Brandon Cesmat's ('99, '01, '04) album of original music *Califor-Noir* was based partly on his books *Driven into the Shade* and *Light in All Directions*.

Elizabeth Chapman's ('92, '93, '00, '04, '07, '09, '11, '15, '18) new chapbook is *Midnight Exhibition at the Wheatgrass Saloon*; she lives in Palo Alto, CA.

Ching-In Chen ('07) is the author of *The Heart's Traffic: a novel in poems* and *recombinant*, which won a Lambda Literary Award for Trans Poetry, and teaches creative writing at University of Washington Bothell.

Nancy Cherry ('91, '04) is the author of the collection *El Verano Burning* and a memoir-in-progress titled *If I Promise to Miss You*, and lives in San Rafael, California.

Brian Cochran ('09, '11, '13, '17) lives in University City, Missouri, and has recent work in *Lana Turner*.

Susan Cohen ('17) is the author of *Throat Singing* and *A Different Wakeful Animal*, has an MFA from Pacific University, and lives in Berkeley, California.

Judy Brackett Crowe ('08, '12, '15, '18, '20) is the author of the chapbook *Flat Water: Nebraska Poems* and lives in Nevada City, California.

Victoria Dalkey ('92), poet and art critic, was a finalist for the Marica and Jan Vilcek Prize for Poetry for her poem "Watching the Olympics on Morphine," which appeared in *Bellevue Literary Review* and was reprinted in the anthology *Quiet Rooms*. She lives in Sacramento, California.

Chris Davidson ('03) lives in Long Beach, California; his chapbook *Easy Meal* (Californios Press) will be published in late 2020.

Armen Davoudian ('18) is the author of *Swan Song*, which won the 2020 Frost Place Chapbook Competition.

Charles Douthat ('04, '09, '12, '14, '20) is a poet, retired litigator, and visual artist whose collection *Blue for Oceans* won the 2010 PEN New England Award as the best book of poetry by a New England author; he lives in Connecticut.

Keith Ekiss ('06) cotranslated *The Fire's Journey* by the Costa Rican poet Eunice Odio, teaches at Stanford University, and lives in San Francisco.

Blas Falconer ('12, '16) is the author of *Forgive the Body This Failure*.

Shangyang Fang ('19) is a Wallace Stegner Fellow at Stanford, and his debut collection is forthcoming from Copper Canyon Press.

Farnaz Fatemi ('14) is cofounder of the Hive Poetry Collective, which produces podcasts and events in Santa Cruz, California, where she works as a writer and editor.

Chanda Feldman ('06) is the author of *Approaching the Fields* and is an assistant professor of creative writing at Oberlin College.

Jay A. Fernandez ('18), whose arts journalism has appeared in the *Washington Post*, *Los Angeles Times*, and *Boston Review*, is also a fiction editor at the *Los Angeles Review of Books*; he lives in South Pasadena, California.

Ann Fisher-Wirth ('92, '00, '09, '13, '20) is the author of six books of poetry, including most recently *The Bones of Winter Birds*; coeditor of *The Ecopoetry Anthology*; and senior fellow of the Black Earth Institute; she directs and teaches in the environmental studies program at the University of Mississippi.

Molly Fisk ('92, '95, '96, '98) edited *California Fire & Water: A Climate Crisis Anthology*, the culmination of her 2019–20 Academy of American Poets Laureate fellowship, and is a writing teacher, radio commentator, and radical life coach in Nevada City, California.

Kevin Fitchett ('14, '19) received a Lucille Clifton Scholarship and a Carlisle Family Scholarship from the Community of Writers, and was a 2020 Provincetown Fine Arts Work Center fellow.

CB Follett ('91, '93, '95, '00, '04), whose most recent book is *Noah's Boat*, coedited *Runes, A Review of Poetry*; was the publisher of Arctos Press; was poet laureate of Marin County from 2010 TO 2013; and lives in Sausalito, California.

Steve Fujimura ('97, '99, '16) lives and works in Berkeley, California.

Cody Gates ('99, '10, '16) has taught poetry, writing, and literature at the University of California, Berkeley and California State University, East Bay.

Beth Kelley Gillogly ('92, '93, '99), a writer and editor living in the Sierra Nevada Foothills, directed the Community of Writers Benefit Poetry Reading for many years.

Jennifer Givhan ('15) is a Mexican American poet who has received NEA and PEN/Rosenthal Emerging Voices fellowships and is the author of two novels and four full-length collections of poetry, most recently *Rosa's Einstein* and *Trinity Sight*.

Veronica Golos ('09) is the author of four poetry books, *A Bell Buried Deep*, *Vocabulary of Silence*, *Rootwork*, and *GIRL*. She is coeditor of the *Taos Journal of International Poetry & Art*.

Hillary Gravendyk ('10) was an associate professor of American poetry at Pomona College in Claremont, California, at the time of her death in 2014, and published three poetry collections, *The Naturalist*, *Harm*, and *The Soluble Hour*, a posthumous volume. The Hilary Gravendyk Prize, sponsored by the Inlandia Institute, was established in her honor.

Leah Naomi Green ('08), the author of *The More Extravagant Feast*, selected by Li-Young Lee for the Walt Whitman Award of the Academy of American Poets, teaches English and environmental studies at Washington and Lee University, and lives in the mountains of Virginia.

Ken Haas ('08, '11, '13, '16, '19, '20) is the author of *Borrowed Light*, works in health care, and sponsors a weekly poetry writing workshop at UCSF Children's Hospital; he lives in San Francisco.

Judy Halebsky ('06, '09, '11, '14), author of three poetry collections, most recently *Spring and a Thousand Years*, directs the low-res MFA in creative writing at Dominican University of California and lives in Oakland.

Forrest Hamer ('92, '97, '02) most recently published the collection *Rift*, has won the Beatrice Hawley and Northern California Book Awards, and lives in Emeryville, California.

John Harvey ('93, '95) is the recipient of honorary doctorates from the Universities of Nottingham and Hertfordshire; an honorary fellow of Goldsmiths College, University of London; and the author most recently of the collection *Aslant*. He lives in London.

Christine Hemp ('06), author of the poetry collection *That Fall* and a memoir, *Wild Ride Home: Love, Loss and a Little White Horse*, lives in Port Townsend, Washington.

Christina Hutchins ('03, '06, '10, '13, '16), author of two collections, *Tender the Maker* (May Swenson Award) and *The Stranger Dissolves*, has worked as a biochemist, Congregational minister, and professor of theology and literary art; has been the Dartmouth poet in residence at the Frost Place; and lives in Albany, California, where she served as the first poet laureate.

Troy Jollimore ('12, '15), whose awards include the National Book Critics Circle Award and a Guggenheim fellowship, is the author of three books of poetry and several works of philosophy.

Alice Jones ('88, '89), the author of *Vault*, *Plunge* (a finalist for the Northern California Book Award in Poetry), and *Gorgeous Mourning*, practices psychoanalysis in Berkeley, California.

Andrew Kaufman ('01, '09) is an NEA recipient residing in New York City; his books include *The Cinnamon Bay Sonnets,* *Earth's Ends, Both Sides of the Niger,* and the forthcoming book *The Rwanda Poems: Voices and Visions from the Genocide.*

Johnny Kovatch ('00) is the author of *59 Hours* and founder of the InsideOUT Writers Prison Insight Program, which is active in California's prison system.

Keetje Kuipers ('05) is the author of three collections of poetry, most recently *All Its Charms,* which contains poems honored with inclusion in the Pushcart Prize and Best American Poetry anthologies; she is the editor of *Poetry Northwest* and lives on Bainbridge Island, Washington, and in Missoula, Montana.

Danusha Laméris ('00) is the author of *The Moons of August* and *Bonfire Opera* and lives in Santa Cruz, California, where she served as poet laureate from 2018 to 2020.

Devi S. Laskar ('04, '08, '14), author of the novel *The Atlas of Reds and Blues* and winner of the 2020 Asian/Pacific American Award in Literature and the 2020 Crook's Corner Book Prize, holds an MFA from Columbia University and lives in Cupertino, California.

Lester Graves Lennon ('99, '01, '03, '05, '07, '09, '11, '13, '15, '17, '19, '20) is poetry editor for *Rosebud* magazine, and his third book, *Lynchings: Postcards from America,* will appear in 2022; he lives in Altadena, California.

Ananda Lima ('17) is the author of *Mother/land,* which will be published in 2021.

Robert Lipton ('94, '03, '18) is the author of the collection *A Complex Bravery* and the winner of the 2018 Gregory O'Donoghue Competition at the Munster Literature Centre in Cork, Ireland, with his poem "Official Story"; he lives in Richmond, California, where he has served as poet laureate.

Jules Mann ('90, '93, '97) helped organize some of the early Community of Writ-

ers Benefit Poetry Reading readings and annual anthologies, until she bunked off in 1998 with her Remington typewriter to live in London, where she directed the UK Poetry Society from 2003 to 2008 and published her chapbook, *Pluck.*

Fred Marchant ('92), the author of *Said Not Said,* founded and directed the Suffolk University Poetry Center in Boston and lives in Arlington, Massachusetts.

Francisco Márquez ('18) is a Venezuelan poet living in Brooklyn, and is the recipient of fellowships from the Fine Arts Work Center in Provincetown, the Poetry Project, and Tin House.

Paco Márquez ('12), author of *Portraits in G Minor,* has published poems in *Fence, Apogee, LiveMag!* and *Huizache.*

Aurora Masum-Javed ('16) is a writer and educator who lives in Spartanburg, South Carolina.

Carrie Allen McCray ('95) started writing later in life and eventually authored three books, *Piece of Time, Freedom's Child: The Life of a Confederate General's Black Child,* and her final one, the posthumous collection *Ota Benga under My Mother's Roof,* edited by Kevin Simmonds and begun at the Community of Writers. At the time of her death in 2008 at age ninety-four, she lived in Columbia, South Carolina.

Sjohnna McCray ('93) is the winner of the 2015 Walt Whitman Award from the Academy of American Poets for his collection *Rapture,* and lives in Athens, Georgia.

Dawn McGuire ('95, '97, '99, '01, '04, '07, '10, '12, '17) is a Bay Area neurologist and the author of four poetry collections, including *The Aphasia Cafe,* winner of the 2012 Indie Poetry Book Prize, and *American Dream with Exit Wound,* a finalist for the 2018 Northern California Book Award.

Meryl Natchez ('87, '88, '00, '05, '09, '13), author of four books, including most recently *Catwalk,* named Best Indie Book for August 2020, is the Marin Poetry Center events manager and lives in Kensington, California.

J. O'Nym ('95, '02) lives in Santa Rosa, California, and is the bassist and vocalist for the band Shimmer; her poem "Survival Suite" appears in the collection *California Fire & Water: A Climate Crisis Anthology*.

Sharon Olson ('97), a retired librarian whose most recent book is *Will There Be Music?*, lives in Lawrenceville, New Jersey.

Yamini Pathak ('18) is the author of the chapbook *Atlas of Lost Places* and the poetry editor for *INCH* magazine, and lives in New Jersey.

Theta Pavis ('99) published most recently in the Emotive Fruition's chapbook *Came with a Clapback* and lives in Jersey City, where she is the director of student media at New Jersey City University.

Emily Pérez ('10, '18), author of *House of Sugar, House of Stone,* and coeditor of *The Long Devotion: Poets Writing Motherhood*, teaches high school and lives in Denver, Colorado.

Lisa Rappoport ('97, '00) most recently published a book of poems, *Penumbra*, and an artist's book, *Liquidambar*, printed letterpress on paper made from leaves of her liquidambar tree in Richmond, California.

Scott Reid ('83, '89) types poems on his Smith Corona manual typewriter at art festivals, fairs, and hospitals; teaches memoir writing at Santa Rosa Junior College; and lives in Monte Rio, California.

Margaret Rhee ('13) was born in Los Angeles and is the author of *Love, Robot*, a collection of science fiction poetry; she is assistant professor in media studies at SUNY Buffalo.

Suzanne Roberts ('04) is the author of four collections of poetry; a memoir, *Almost Somewhere: Twenty-Eight Days on the John Muir Trail*; and a collection of travel essays, *Bad Tourist: Misadventures in Love and Travel*. She lives in South Lake Tahoe, California.

Michelle Brittan Rosado ('16), author of *Why Can't It Be Tenderness*, which won the 2018 Felix Pollak Poetry Prize, teaches at the University of Southern California and lives in Long Beach, California.

Renato Rosaldo ('00, '02, '07) has published four books of poetry, most recently *The Chasers* (Duke University Press).

Lois Rosen ('99, '01, '20) leads the Trillium Writers and ICL Writing Workshop at Willamette University, cofounded the Peregrine Writers, won the Kay Snow 2016 Fiction Contest, published poetry most recently in *Calyx*, and lives in Salem, Oregon.

Yiskah Rosenfeld ('01, '03, '19) was a finalist for the 2019 Slippery Elm Prize; has poems forthcoming in *The Bitter Oleander*, *Tikkun*, and *Wild Gods: The Ecstatic in Contemporary Poetry and Lyrical Prose*; and lives in Albany, California.

Elizabeth Rosner ('99) is the author of *Gravity*, a poetry collection, as well as three novels and a book of nonfiction; she leads writing workshops internationally and resides in Berkeley, California.

Deborah Dashow Ruth's ('01, '02, '05, '08, '00, '01, '05, '08, '13, '17) first collection of poetry, *Joyriding on an Updraft*, was published in 2015; she lives in Kensington, California.

Larry Ruth ('00, '13, '16, '20) coauthored (with Scott L. Stephens) an article in *Ecological Applications* titled "Federal Forest Fire Policy in the United States;" he consults in environmental and forest policy, and lives in Berkeley, California.

Cintia Santana ('14, '17) teaches literary translation and poetry and fiction workshops in Spanish at Stanford University; as a member of Right Window Gallery in San Francisco, she creates poetry-based window installations.

Eliot Schain's ('98, '02, '07, '16) new collection is *The Distant Sound*.

Alix Anne Shaw ('10) is the author of *Rough Ground*, winner of the Lexi Rudnitsky Poetry Prize, and a resident of Milwaukee, Wisconsin.

Thandiwe Shiphrah ('00), a multidisciplinary artist, lives in Nashville, Tennessee, and founded the Line Breaks Literary Reading Series.

Maurya Simon's ('84) newest book is *The Wilderness: New and Selected Poems* (2018); she is a professor emerita at the University of California, Riverside and lives in the Angeles National Forest.

giovanni singleton ('96, '04, '09) authored *Ascension* and the poetry/art collection *AMERICAN LETTERS: works on paper*, which won the California Book Award for Poetry and received the African American Literature and Culture Society's Stephen E. Henderson Award; she lives in Fairfax, California.

Jen Siraganian ('12, '14) is a Pushcart Prize nominee and the author of the chapbook *Fracture*, and her poems have appeared in *Best New Poets 2016*, *Mid-American Review*, *Barrow Street*, and other publications; she lives in the Santa Cruz Mountains.

Monica Sok ('15), a Cambodian American poet, and author of *A Nail the Evening Hangs On*, is a Jones Lecturer at Stanford University who teaches poetry to Southeast Asian youths at the Center for Empowering Refugees and Immigrants in Oakland.

Mary Austin Speaker ('06) is the author of *Ceremony* and *The Bridge* and lives in Minneapolis, Minnesota, where she is the art director for Milkweed Editions.

Elizabeth Sullivan ('02, '05, '10, '13), a poet and psychotherapist in private practice whose work has appeared in *Poems & Plays*, *Fourteen Hills*, *Poem* literary magazine, and several other publications, lives in San Francisco and in Sydney, Australia.

Karen A. Terrey ('06, '12, '15, '17), the author of the chapbook *Bite and Blood*, has poems in *Kokanee*, *Rhino*, *Meadow*, *WordRiot*, *Puerto del Sol*, *Canary*, and *Grey Sparrow Journal*; teaches at Sierra College; and lives in Truckee, California.

Amber Flora Thomas ('92, '02, '04, '13) is the author of three poetry collections: *Eye of Water*, *The Rabbits Could Sing*, and *Red Channel in the Rupture*. She lives in Washington, North Carolina.

Robert Thomas ('88), whose most recent book, *Bridge*, received the 2015 PEN Center USA Literary Award for Fiction, lives in Oakland, California.

Vickie Vértiz ('15), most recently published in *McSweeney's* and whose collection *Palm Frond with Its Throat Cut* won the 2018 PEN America Literary Award in Poetry, lives in Los Angeles and teaches at the University of California, Santa Barbara.

Marci Vogel ('07, '17) is a California-born poet and the author of *Death and Other Holidays* and *At the Border of Wilshire & Nobody*.

Benjamin Voigt ('19) grew up on a small farm and the internet. He works as an academic technologist at Macalester College and lives in Minneapolis with his wife and poodle.

Valerie Wallace ('10), author of *House of McQueen*, which was the winner of the Four Way Books Intro Prize and named one of the best poetry books of 2018 by the *Chicago Review of Books*, lives in Chicago.

Charles Harper Webb ('91) has published twelve collections of poetry, including *Sidebend World*; teaches at California State University, Long Beach; and lives in Glendale, California.

Maw Shein Win ('02), author of *Score and Bone*, *Invisible Gifts: Poems*, and *Storage Unit for the Spirit House*, was the inaugural poet laureate of El Cerrito, California, and lives and teaches in the San Francisco Bay Area.

Sholeh Wolpé ('04) is the author of over twelve collections of poetry, literary translations, and anthologies, as well as several plays, and is the writer-in-residence at the University of California, Irvine.

Shelley Wong ('16) is the author of *As She Appears*, winner of the Pamet River Prize, and is an affiliate artist at Headlands Center for the Arts; she has received fellowships from Kundiman and MacDowell Colony, and lives in San Francisco.

Sondra Zeidenstein ('90, '91, '92, '94, '01) was a poet and a teacher of English literature, and was the founding editor and publisher of Chicory Blue Press, which specialized in poetry by older women writers. She passed away in 2020.

Editors

Lisa Alvarez ('91, '93) became Co-Director of the Writers Workshops in 1999 and has also worked as Assistant to the Poetry Director since then. Coeditor of *Orange County: A Literary Field Guide*, Alvarez is a professor at Irvine Valley College and lives in Modjeska Canyon, California.

Laura Howard is a Publishing Consultant for the Community of Writers and has worked for nonprofits and publications such as *Tin House*, *Voice of Witness*, *The Believer/McSweeney's*, and *ZYZZYVA* for over twenty-five years; she lives in San Francisco.

Brett Hall Jones, who has led the Community of Writers since 1991, was raised in Olympic Valley and the summer workshops by Community of Writers cofounders Barbara and Oakley Hall. She is married to novelist Louis B. Jones, codirector of Community of Writers' fiction program. Also a photographer, in recent years she has concentrated on portraits of poets and writers.

Eva Melas is the Director of Alumni Relations and Development for the Community of Writers and lives in Grass Valley, California.